What people are saying about …

Secondhand Jesus

"Digging through the ruins of a 'house built on sand,' Glenn Packiam lays bare the shameless lies of a way of religion that is without foundations in Jesus or Scripture. But it is far more than exposé. This is an honest, personal, detailed story of a Christian leader refusing cynicism and embracing forgiveness and hope."

Eugene H. Peterson, professor emeritus of Spiritual Theology, Regent College, Vancouver, B.C., Canada

"Glenn Packiam is not only a gifted songwriter and worship leader, penning songs that capture the heart of our generation, but he is also a gifted writer whose textured voice needs to be heard. *Secondhand Jesus* is a much-needed challenge for every believer to embrace knowing God like they never have before."

Margaret Feinberg, popular speaker and author of *Scouting the Divine*

"Glenn Packiam is an authentic Christ-follower, and as his pastor, I am privileged to watch him teach and lead others on this journey to having a firsthand faith in Jesus. This book is a must-read for anyone wanting more in their walk with Jesus."

Brady Boyd, senior pastor, New Life Church

"What a great read! Page after page I found myself hooked. Glenn has written a book that not only engaged my mind, but also made my heart beat faster for Jesus."

David Nasser, author and speaker

"Glenn Packiam offers a personal and thoughtful exploration of the rumors and misconceptions that have plagued the Christian faith. It is a must-read for anyone whose faith has become stale or apathetic, but it also offers something for even the most earnest of believers—a challenge to infuse one's faith with a firsthand relationship with God."

Rob Stennett, author of *The Almost True Story of Ryan Fisher* and *The End Is Now*

"In this refreshingly honest look at the authentic faith of Jesus, Glenn Packiam pulls back the curtain to reveal secondhand versions of a consumer-driven Christianity that portrays God as a vending machine and the church as a trade show for superficial solutions to gut-wrenching realities. Instead Packiam invites us to exchange easy answers for the startling reality of a God who is not afraid of impolite questions and a Jesus who invites us beyond rumors to a firsthand faith with the power to redeem us in the real world. Engaging, accessible, and profound, this is a book for veterans and novices alike who want to stop pretending with religion and start getting real with God."

Bob Rognlien, lead pastor of Lutheran Church of the Good Shepherd and author of *Experiential Worship*

Secondhand Jesus

Trading rumors of God for a firsthand faith.

Secondhand Jesus

Trading rumors of God for a firsthand faith.

GLENN PACKIAM

David C Cook®

transforming lives together

SECONDHAND JESUS
Published by David C. Cook
4050 Lee Vance View
Colorado Springs, CO 80918 U.S.A.

David C. Cook Distribution Canada
55 Woodslee Avenue, Paris, Ontario, Canada N3L 3E5

David C. Cook U.K., Kingsway Communications
Eastbourne, East Sussex BN23 6NT, England

The Web site addresses recommended throughout this book are offered as a
resource to you. These Web sites are not intended in any way to be or imply an
endorsement on the part of David C. Cook, nor do we vouch for their content.

LCCN 2009924472
ISBN 978-1-4347-6639-7
eISBN 978-1-4347-0032-2

© 2009 Glenn Packiam

The Team: John Blase, Amy Kiechlin, Jaci Schneider, and Caitlyn York
Cover Design and Illustration by Jon Egan

Printed in the United States of America
First Edition 2009

2 3 4 5 6 7 8 9 10

070709

To my wife,
for refusing shortcuts and persisting
on the long, bloody walk with God.
You inspire me.

To Aaron and Jossie,
for showing me how to wrestle
with God through the darkest night.

Contents

Acknowledgments

All through Israel's history—and particularly their early, nomadic history—faithful people built altars to God. Altars are a place of worship, a visible memorial of God's faithfulness on a particular occasion. Noah, Abraham, Isaac, Jacob, Moses, Joshua, Gideon, Samuel, Saul, David, Elijah—and many others—built altars to God. Like carvings in a tree or graffiti on a wall in our day, their altars were a way of saying, "God was here." In wilderness and in war, in provision and in confusion, God was in their midst.

As I've written this book, I've realized it has been a sort of memorial stone, an altar to what God has done in my life these past few years. But the way God has been present has not always been in ways I would have expected. In hindsight, I can see that God has been present through the people around me. They are fellow pilgrims and living reminders of God's faithfulness. They are the ones to whom I owe my deepest debt. So here it goes.

To Ross Parsley—a church could not find a more faithful and humble man, and a man could not find a better friend. You are the reason. You are the catalyst.

To Brady Boyd—thanks for taking the risk on what you believed to be a "kingdom assignment" and what I know to be God's grace to our church. You are a genuine man of God and a gracious leader.

To my brothers-in-arms, my friends and fellow young pastors— our friendship began on mountaintops, but our bond was forged in the valley.

To my so-called "nonpastor" friends—thanks for never believing that knowing God was the sole property of "professional ministers."

To the staff at New Life Worship, New Life School of Worship, and theMILL—thanks for being incredible teammates and being patient with me as I've learned to be the same. I'm grateful to be in this with you.

To Don Pape—this would not have happened without you. I am deeply grateful for your belief in me and for all the breakfasts at Cracker Barrel.

To John Blase—thank you for your time, attention, insight, and encouragement.

To Doug Mann and the team at Cook—you are terrific to work with. Let's do it again!

To my parents—you have been my compass. Thank you for giving me a home built on the Rock and for helping me find my way back to it.

To Holly, my dear wife—your passion for the Bible and your diligence in prayer and reading have not let me devolve into laziness and inaction. Thank you for making me a better man. To our girls, Sophia and Norah—your beauty and joy have been my light in some very dark days.

Because of all of you, I can say, like Jacob after he awoke from seeing the heavens open and angels ascending and descending, "Surely the LORD is in this place, and I was not aware of it" (Gen 28:16).

Foreword

This year I celebrate twenty years of being a pastor, if *celebrate* is the right word. Much of those twenty years have been, as Paul puts it, travail, birth pains, pouring myself out like a drink offering, carrying around in my body the death of Jesus, filling up in my flesh what is lacking in regard to Christ's afflictions.

Or at least, that's how it's felt to me.

But I've also visited churches far and very different from my own (and some within minutes of where I live but which may as well be continents away), and a dim awareness is emerging. I've met pastors whose pay scale and working conditions and daily rounds make me look like the captain of a cruise ship (and sometimes merely like a passenger on one), and it's slowly dawning on me that maybe being inconvenienced and slightly underpaid for the gospel's sake isn't what the Bible means by tribulation.

I've a growing hunch that these past twenty years have been, for me, very comfortable indeed.

Secondhand Jesus serves up a strong confirmation of that hunch, and a stiff rebuke to it. Not that the book's about pastoring. It's about Jesus, and about the church in North America, and about how the two sometimes fail to meet. It's a clear-eyed and unflinching look at how Christians, pastors included, miss Jesus and misrepresent Him. It's a ruthless and yet loving critique of how often we, with all the best of intentions, redefine what it means to know Jesus and worship Him alone.

Glenn woke up the hard way, which is the way most of us wake up. He's part of the pastoral staff of one of the most "successful" churches anywhere, ever. But one day, without warning, that church was swept up in a tempest of scandal, and soon after in a whirlwind of tragedy. Glenn wondered if the church would survive. He fretted about his job security. He worried about not being able to make his mortgage payments.

But then a deeper reality began to surface: Had he, had the church, missed and misrepresented Jesus? Had the lure and glamour of success eclipsed the beauty of Christ, the man of sorrows familiar with suffering? Had an American Idol culture within the church displaced the humble King?

Hardship and heartbreak forced on Glenn a profound reevaluation. Secondhand Jesus is the fruit of that reevaluation. This is much more than a chronicle of events, though it includes enough of that to help us ground Glenn's journey in real time. This is a rich work of biblical excavation. Glenn mines the many stories of the ark of the covenant—that long-lost, much-sought, legend-laden, gold-plated box featured in the early exploits of Israel's history. This was the box that Israel carried through the desert and across the Jordan. It was the box that they took to war—their seemingly secret weapon of mass destruction. It was the prize and then the bane of Israel's enemies, the Philistines. It was the box over which the priest Uzzah lost his life, and the box before which David danced. It was the box that resided, until it was plundered, in the Holy of Holies.

The ark weaves in and out of Scripture, comprising a collection of intriguing, exotic, somewhat enigmatic stories. But in Glenn's hands, those stories serve as lenses both to focus and magnify our culture's discontents, our strange amalgam of superstition, shallow piety, wishful and magical thinking—in a word, our "God in a Box" syndrome. They become indictments and correctives to our own self-serving theologies.

But this book is not a tirade. It's no self-righteous harangue against modern innovations followed by a stern call to return to that "old time" religion. It's more a confession and a plea. It's a bone-deep admission of personal failure, a heartfelt repentance for that failure, and a soul-stirring call to put aside childish things and to seek first the kingdom of God and His righteousness.

It's honest and forthright. It's inspiring and convicting. It confronts, and it invites.

In fact, it's helped me set a few things aright—to stop missing and misrepresenting Christ. And it's given me hope that, even if these past twenty years have been mostly comfortable, these next twenty might be infinitely better—which is to say, all for Jesus.

- –Mark Buchanan,
pastor of New Life Community Baptist
Church in Duncan, British Columbia,
and author of *Your God Is Too Safe*

1. Thursday

Life couldn't have been any better. We had been in our new house for just over a year, and it was almost time to start decorating for the holidays. Winter's frost was just blowing in over the Rocky Mountains. These were days of sipping hot chocolate and looking back over a year of steady church growth, rapidly expanding influence, and a company of close friends to enjoy it with. On top of all that, my wife, Holly, and I were expecting our second child, another girl. Life was good and there was no end in sight.

And then it was Thursday.

Everyone was distracted at work. There were meetings going on, first upstairs and then off campus, and later on campus in an impromptu staff meeting. Internet clips kept us glued to the screen as we tried desperately to decipher truth, accuracy, and some reason to believe the best. But as Thursday soldiered on, doubt was sitting lower and more heavily inside me.

I remember the feeling when I got home. My heart was kicking against my chest with frantic irregularity as I ran up the stairs to our room. The tightening knot in my stomach seemed to sink with each step. I opened our bedroom door, and with breathless shock sputtered, "Babe, some of it's true."

I had just returned from an elders' meeting where I learned that the seemingly absurd accusations leveled against our beloved pastor had enough truth in them to warrant his removal from office. On Friday, we learned that he would never be allowed back. By Sunday, we were sitting in church with hot tears racing down our faces, listening to letters that told us words we never thought we would hear. Our pastor had been a prominent national figure because of his role as president of the National Association of Evangelicals. He had been featured on Barbara Walters' program and other major news shows, had been called the most influential pastor in America. It was the biggest religious debacle in my lifetime. And it happened at my church. My church.

Thursday came and everything changed; my unshakeable "good life" became a nightmare of uncertainty. Would the church implode? Would everyone leave? Would I have a job next week? Could I ever get hired in ministry again? The songs, the influence, the success, the notoriety—it all became foolishly irrelevant.

Slowly, I replayed the past. The preceding years had been heady times. Our pastor's meteoric rise to the evangelical papacy paralleled the growing muscle of a conservative Christian movement now beginning to flex in the public square. The young men who had helped build our church, myself included, now found themselves swimming in much bigger circles of influence. We were talking to the press, traveling to Washington DC, and dropping more names than Old Testament genealogy. We had become powerful by association. And it was intoxicating. We were like the eager young men in Tobias Wolff's fictitious memoir of an elite prep school on the eastern seaboard, full of idealism and world-changing dreams.

It was a good dream and we tried to live it out, even while knowing that we were actors in a play, and that outside the theater was a world we would have to reckon with when the curtain closed and the doors were flung open.[1]

On Thursday, the theater doors flung open. The dream was over now. There was no thought of making an impact or changing the world. It was now about survival. How could we help our church stay intact?

As the days became weeks, it became clear that our church was made up of strong families who truly were connected to each other. It is a community akin to a small Midwestern town. So what if the mayor is gone? We're all still here. I watched men and women rally together in a heroic display of Christlike love.

It wasn't long before the shock of scandal gave way to the discomfort of introspection. This was ultimately not about a fallen pastor; it was about fallen nature, a nature we all have lurking within us. It became less about the worst being true about him, and more about the worst being true about us. We began to allow the Lord to turn His spotlight, one more piercing than the light of any cameras, on our own hearts. Secret sins, recurring temptations, and hidden pride all looked sinister in His light. There was no such thing as a little white anything. Every weakness was now a dangerous monster with the potential of ruining our lives. Couples began to have difficult conversations with each other, friends became more vulnerable than they had ever been. Honest was the new normal. That sounds so strange to say.

But far beyond discussions and confessions, one question, one I never thought I would have trouble answering, relentlessly worked its way to my core. It surfaced from the pages of Henri Nouwen's book *In the Name of Jesus*. Nouwen had been an influential theology professor at Harvard, living at what most would have considered the apex of his career. But something was wrong.

> *After twenty years in the academic world as a teacher of pastoral psychology, pastoral theology, and Christian spirituality, I began to experience a deep inner threat. As I entered into my fifties ... I came face to face with the simple question, "Did becoming older bring me closer to Jesus?" After twenty-five years of priesthood, I found myself praying poorly, living somewhat isolated from other people, and very much preoccupied with burning issues.*[2]

But Nouwen's inner wrestling was largely unnoticed by those around him, which made it more difficult for him to accurately gauge the condition of his heart.

Everyone was saying that I was doing really well, but something inside was telling me that my success was putting my own soul in danger. I began to ask myself whether my lack of contemplative prayer, my loneliness, and my constantly changing involvement in what seemed most urgent were signs that the Spirit was gradually being suppressed ... I was living in a very dark place and ... the term "burnout" was a convenient psychological translation for spiritual death.[3]

Haunted by the emptiness of his own spiritual walk, Nouwen started on a journey that eventually led to his resignation from Harvard. He took a position as a chaplain at L'Arche, a care facility for the handicapped. There he learned what it meant to live out a life of love and servanthood, to live as Christ among the broken, to truly "lead in the name of Jesus." I had read his profound and honest reflections years before, but as I reread them in the wake of the scandal, I found myself convicted. Nouwen's question dealt with something deeper than sin; it was about the essence of the Christian life, the thing we must have above all else.

I remember sitting with a few friends in my living room on New Year's Eve, reflecting on how insane 2006 had been. We decided to have a little dessert and ponder the year that was now in its closing hours. Each couple took turns reviewing highs and lows of the year. For the most part, it had been a good year. Bigger and better opportunities, unexpected financial success, the births of healthy children, and the accelerated elimination of debt were some of the items on the good list. But we had also experienced Thursday, and "bigger and better" now seemed as days long ago, *auld lang syne.* The events of that day in November now overshadowed everything the next year might hold. Everything was good now, but how long would it continue? Would the things that had gone awry last year create repercussions that would undermine all the things we had held so dearly? For some, the fear of losing the jobs they loved was becoming a distinct possibility. The reality of how suddenly a curve in the road can appear was sobering us.

And then I raised The Question: Did we—did I—know Christ more as a result of the passing of another year? Were we any closer to God? It was not the sort of question to answer out loud. I wrestled with it in silence. It was a question of my own relationship with Christ.

I have been a Christian since I was a young boy. I spent my high school years sitting in on the Old Testament history classes my mom taught at our church's Bible college, listening to sermon tapes, and praying and planning with my dad as he and my mom planted a church. My youth was defined by long quiet times, meaningful journal entries, and leadership roles in our youth group. I was a theology major in college and had been in full-time, vocational ministry for six years. Yet in the wake of Thursday, none of this mattered. Did I truly know God ... *today?* Was my knowledge of Him active and alive, or stale and sentimental?

There was no easy or succinct way to answer that question. But as I allowed it to burrow its way in my heart, I began to see something. I had long lived subconsciously believing that God was a sort of cosmic agent, working to get me bigger contracts and better deals while saving me from scammers and opportunists. God was my Jerry Maguire, my ambassador of quan, and my prayers were spiritually cloaked

versions of asking Him to "show me the money." Not necessarily
literal money—just comfort, success, good friends, an enjoyably
smooth road, an unmitigated path to the peak of my game.

If you had suggested that theology to me, I would have con-
demned it, criticized it, and denied three times that I even knew
of it. It wasn't until Thursday came and went that I saw what was
lurking inside. I had slowly bought the suburban rumors of God.
My house was an evidence of His blessing. Our growing church was
an indication of God's pleasure. Things were going to get better and
better while I kept my life on cruise control. Never mind that I had
struggled—mostly unsuccessfully—to have consistent time alone
with God. Forget that I had hardly spent time worshipping God
offstage.

The more my wife and I searched our own souls, the more we
realized we had become passive, complacent, at times even indiffer-
ent about our own knowledge of God. We had been lulled to sleep
by our own apparent success, numbed into coasting by our spiritual
Midas touch.

What began in the days after Thursday was a journey, a road of
uncovering and discovering, of stripping away what thoughts of God
we now knew were rumors and finding again the face of Christ.

These were not rumors that came from one man, one pastor. In
fact, it's hard to say that any of them did. Any search for the head-
waters would be misguided anyway. Because that's not the point. It's
not *where* the rumors came from; it's *why* they came at all.

Here's what I've learned: Rumors grow in the absence of revelation. Every time we keep God at arm's length, declining an active,
living knowledge of Him, we become vulnerable to rumors. Lulled

by false comfort and half-truths about God, we—in Keith Green's famous words—fall asleep in the light.

What the Heck is Going On?

Until life comes to a screeching halt.

There are moments when time stands still. Our old vision of the world, like a scrim on a giant set, rolls up out of sight, leaving us with a jagged, stark picture of reality, its edges sharp, rough, and bare. Everything looks different, feels different. Things that once peppered our lives with meaning are now completely irrelevant and vain. Things we had ignored and overlooked are now incredibly clear, almost stunning in the forefront. The football team whose games you would never miss now seems horridly trivial. The powerful boss you were trying to impress, you now scorn and dismiss. The child you once wished would just go to sleep, you now run to hold in your arms.

A death of a loved one, the finality of divorce, the weight of debt crushing into bankruptcy—these are the moments that shake us, that wake us up and make us numb all at the same time. My moment is not that tragic in light of others. I think of a friend whose wife is facing a medically incurable disease. Or another friend whose wife decided married life was overrated and the party scene was where she belonged. I know a father who can't escape the grief of losing a child years ago. Sorrow covers him like a cape and time offers no oxygen. There is no way to compare tragic moments. The game of my-moment-is-worse-than-your-moment, while possible, is seldom profitable. Pain is acutely real to those who are breaking under its weight.

These are the "what the heck?" moments. The moments where everything stops except you, as you slowly look around. Examining. Reflecting. Puzzled. Bewildered. The silence is broken by a bellow from deep inside: "What the heck is going on?" Or some less sanitized version of the same. How could this be? And what's more, how could this be while God is with me?

The psalmists understood this feeling well. Fully two-thirds of Psalms are laments, an old-fashioned term for a "what the heck?" moment prayer. Imagine these words being prayed at church:

Why, O LORD, do you stand far off? Why do you hide yourself in times of trouble? (Ps. 10:1)

My God, my God, why have you forsaken me? Why are you so far from saving me, so far from the words of my groaning? O my God, I cry out by day, but you do not answer, by night, and am not silent. (Ps. 22:1–2)

My tears have been my food day and night, while men say to me all day long, "Where is your God?" (Ps. 42:3)

These were covenant people, people to whom God had made an unbreakable promise, a promise to bless them, protect them, and make their days go well. So why on earth were they being pursued by enemies, losing their belongings, and getting depressed—all while watching the wicked flourish? It didn't make sense. It wasn't lining up with the covenant—or at least their understanding of it. And so they took their complaint up with God.

What's interesting is that, for the most part, we don't find out how God specifically responded. There are "psalms of Thanksgiving," where the psalmist restates his lament in the past tense—recounting how he was in trouble—and then gives thanks to God for delivering him. But the "lament psalms" grossly outnumber the "thanksgiving psalms." We don't know if all became well on earth all the time. But we are told two crucial things: the consistent character of God—good, just, faithful, loving—and the characteristic response of the psalmists—the choice to praise. In one of the psalms quoted earlier, the words of lament are followed by these words of praise:

> *Yet you are enthroned as the Holy One; you are the praise of Israel. (Ps. 22:3)*

Maybe in some ways, the Bible is written the way the Oracle in *The Matrix* prophesies: It only tells us what we need to know. It does not tell us all there is to know, only what we need for life and godliness. Here is the lesson of the psalmists: All of our experiences and emotions can become a springboard to find God and see Him for ourselves. God is present on every scene, waiting, wanting us to seek Him, believe in Him, and worship Him with every ounce of our existence.

Our discussion here is not first about suffering. The question of whether God causes it, allows it, or has nothing to do with it, has been voiced since the days in the garden. Our discussion here is simply that these moments—whether they come from our free will, the Devil's evil schemes, or God's strange providence—present us with an opportunity. Regardless of your theology, these two things are common to mankind: We all experience a measure of suffering, and every experience can be redeemed.

C. S. Lewis wrote, "God whispers to us in our pleasures, speaks in our conscience, but shouts in our pain: it is His megaphone to rouse a deaf world."[4]

Crumbs of Rumor

Too often, we walk through life with our hands fixed firmly over our eyes and ears, ignoring and avoiding the living presence of Christ with us—maybe from fear or guilt or simple apathy. But every once in awhile, our hands are pried off our faces, our eyes are almost forcibly opened, our ears are unplugged. We catch a glimpse for ourselves, a glimpse that will be our undoing. And our salvation. In that moment, we are ruined and redeemed by that little glimpse.

Job had that experience.

He never auditioned for the role, never signed up for the part. God chose him. He chose him, we are often told, to prove a point to the Devil. But I'm beginning to wonder if God chose him to show Himself to Job, to save Job from the stiff, straight lines he had drawn around God. Think about it. The story doesn't end with the Devil returning to heaven and saying, "Okay, God, You win. You were right. Job didn't curse You. He does indeed serve You for nothing in return." If that were the central tension in the story, there is a glaring lack of resolution.

A series of ridiculously unfortunate events befalls Job in a very short span of time. What takes place in the lengthy remainder of the book is a dialogue between Job, three of his friends, and a presumptuously precocious young man named Elihu. After sitting silently for seven days, the three friends can't bear to hold in their wisdom. One by one they present their cases to Job, trying to explain why he is suffering and what he should do about it. They generally agree that things have gone so poorly for Job because of some hidden sin in his life. They plead with him to go before God, repent, rid himself of his sins, and make peace with the Almighty. Job refuses. He insists on his innocence and laments to God with words that are uncomfortably honest.

Then Elihu speaks. He dismisses the elders' wisdom, preferring his own fresh insight. He is less willing to condemn Job for sin, but not as reluctant to rebuke him for pride. He hints at God's sovereignty and our inability to fully understand His ways. But he, too, echoes the familiar refrain that obedience will lead to a prosperous, pleasant life, and that disobedience will lead to tragedy and sorrow.

As arrogant and simpleminded as Job's friends may seem to us, as hard as it is to imagine ourselves saying something like that to a friend who has just lost everything, remember that they are simply articulating the prevailing wisdom of the day. It was their misguided understanding of the covenant that gave them this simple premise: Obey God, and all will be well; disobey, and you will suffer.

That formulaic and faulty view of the covenant may be the reason the book of Job is included in Hebrew Wisdom Literature. It may be that the purpose for the book of Job is to counter an overly black-and-white view of life. Perhaps God understood that humans would take the rich, profoundly unique covenant that He had made with His people and reduce it to simplistic, pithy phrases. Maybe God knows our propensity to redact the living words of relationship into rumors that spread like fire—and that sooner or later, we will get burned.

What if the book of Job is not all about some intergalactic dispute between God and the Devil? What if it's really about revelation and relationship with mortals?

At the end of the story, after Job asks God over and over with the nagging persistence of a two-year-old why he has suffered, God responds. Not with answers, but with questions—questions that bring Job to his knees. Finally Job cries:

> *I admit I once lived by rumors of you; now I have it all*
> *firsthand—from my own eyes and ears! I'm sorry—forgive*
> *me. I'll never do that again, I promise! I'll never again live on*
> *crusts of hearsay, crumbs of rumor. (Job 42:5–6 MSG)*

This is the climax of the book of Job. It's the way this incredibly moving story of suffering resolves. The mention of God restoring to Job more than what he lost is sort of an afterthought, a footnote to the story. It comes after Job finds firsthand knowledge of God. The story of Job is first and foremost a salvation story: God saved Job from small, narrow, rumor-laden views of Himself. And then Job lived holy-ever-after. It's what happens when rumors give way to revelation.

I have come to the uncomfortable realization that I have believed rumors about God that have kept me from Him, kept me from really knowing Him. I suspect I am not alone. This book is about some of the more popular rumors and the path to finding the truth. What you read here is not intended to be the basis for your view of God.

Instead, this book is an attempt to jog your mind, stir your heart, provoke your questions, and whet your appetite for the quest, for the journey that only you can take. The journey that Job took. A journey that is not necessarily one of suffering, but one that by design means eye-opening, paradigm-shattering discovery. So yes, in some sense it hurts. It's a journey that begins with your fist to the sky and can end with your knees on the earth. A journey that begins with questions and ends with speechless worship.

Mine began on a Thursday.

DISCUSSION QUESTIONS:

1. What are some of your "what the heck?" moments?

2. Do you think your knowledge of Christ is active and alive or stale and sentimental?

3. What are you looking for God to do in your heart as you read this book?

2. Rumors

I heard a story the other day that was quite disturbing.

A man awoke to the buzzing sound of an unfamiliar alarm. As he glanced at the glowing red numbers, he slowly became aware of his surroundings. The giant floral print on the comforter was not what he remembered picking out with his wife. The curtains were thicker, somehow better at keeping out the light than the ones in his bedroom. *This isn't my room.*

It was the smell of leftover food that finally prodded his mind. *I'm at a hotel.* And then it hit him. *I'm late!*

His flight was scheduled to leave in about sixty minutes. He sprang out of bed, threw on his clothes, and hurriedly crammed the few items he had brought with him into his roll-on suitcase before running out the hotel door. Fortunately, he was at an airport hotel and there was still time to catch the shuttle. *I can't miss this flight. I've got to get home.* He was so preoccupied with getting the shuttle driver to understand the urgency of his situation that it wasn't until he was fumbling in his coat pocket for a tip that he realized something was missing. The hotel key card. He had kept it in there yesterday hoping to remember to turn it in at the front desk. It had been his first hotel stay in a long time, and he wasn't sure if failure to turn in your key would result in a fine.

Too late to worry about it now. He must have left it in the room. Perhaps one of the housekeeping staff would find it and turn it in.

By lunchtime the next day, he knew something was wrong when the waiter asked if there was another credit card he'd like to use. Later that afternoon, his wife called wondering why her card had failed at the grocery store. Frantic, they called their credit card company only to have their fears confirmed: They were the victims of identity fraud. Their cards were maxed and their credit badly flawed.

As it turned out, the hotel, as matter of standard procedure, had embedded his credit card number, expiration date, and full name on the magnetic strip of the key card. Somehow, it must have gotten into the wrong hands. Someone had used the card to extract his information and then gone on a massive online spending spree.

Needless to say, when I heard the story I was paranoid. As a frequent traveler, I can't remember how many times I've left hotel key cards in the room. I know a friend who saves every key card from every hotel he's ever visited. I dismissed it as a quirky souvenir idea, but maybe he's the smarter man for it. At least his credit card information isn't floating out there.

But the truth is, neither is mine.

The "embedded credit card information on a hotel key card" story is one of the more popular urban legends of our time, particularly among road warriors. The rumor began in 2003 when a member of the Pasadena Police Department started circulating an e-mail warning of dangers she believed were real. She had been in a briefing meeting with other fraud detectives and learned there that one detective had encountered a hotel key card with personal credit card information on it. The detectives had not yet determined if it was standard procedure for hotels to embed personal information on their key cards. Nevertheless, alarmed at the possibility of rampant identity fraud, she wrote her e-mail, intended as a sort of "heads-up" to other detectives.

The e-mail, and the rumor in it, took on a life of its own and has been filling the hearts of travelers with fear ever since.

What we now know is that it is not standard procedure for hotels to embed any personal information on their key cards. Furthermore, in 2006, Computerworld did a study of one hundred different hotel key cards and reached two significant conclusions: First, hardly any information on the cards was readable by standard off-the-shelf card readers; secondly, even sophisticated, professional card readers could not detect any personal information.[1] Sources within the hotel industry insist that while the technology exists for them to embed credit card information on the key cards, it would be at an additional cost to them and would provide no perceivable benefit. After all, your credit card information is already on their computers.

The haunting problem with this urban legend and its unsettling conclusion—and maybe the reason it is still alive and well—is simply this: It could happen. It could be true.

The most dangerous of rumors are the ones that contain an element of truth, a twinge of possibility. They are just believable enough to keep us dangling in fear, hanging in anticipation. They resemble reality just enough to hold us hostage. And every time we try to escape into the light of reason and common sense, they jerk us back into our dungeon with a thought that grips us more tightly than a hangman's noose: It could be true. And I could be wrong.

What If It's True?

It is a terrible thing to be wrong. Nobody likes finding out that something they had been doing, some routine or ritual, habit or practice, was dreadfully wrong in some way. Nobody wants to hear that a long-held belief was finally proven to be false.

Ironically, it's this fear of being wrong that causes us to entertain rumors. We're afraid that others know something that we don't, and we don't want to be left in the dark. We second-guess our vanilla, mainstream life choices. What if there's more and I didn't know it? What if I'm missing out? When a partially informed friend passes on some tip or tidbit of truth, our ears perk to attention. Is there really a way to win a free iPod on the Internet? Is Microsoft really giving away money? Is that stock really going to double in a month? It's not the inherent plausibility of the rumor that sucks us in; it's the sheer fact that if it were somehow, someway true and we failed to act that we would have missed out. We would be left to lament our own skepticism. If only we would have stopped being such doubters.

And so we take the risk. We explore the possibility of truth. The more we hear others saying the same thing we've heard, the more credibility is added to our hope. *See, they've heard it too. Maybe it's true.* You stake your bid on hearsay, albeit very popular hearsay.

Eat only high-protein meat and lose weight!

Juice every fruit and vegetable you've ever heard of and even some you haven't heard of and cure your ailments!

Fish meat has everything you need to become healthy and smart!

And then one day it comes crashing down. The roof that sat lofty on Certainty's walls now rests in Reality's basement. Truth taunts us for even trying to reach the sky with our house of cards.

You discover that your body needs whole grains to properly process meat. You realize you've been consuming more sugar in a glass of juice than you would have in a day's worth of meals. It occurs to you that if you would never sit down and eat ten oranges, why would drinking the juice from them be okay? You learn that too much mercury—found in an alarming number of fish—can actually shut down your brain's best functions.

The very thing you were trying to avoid when you began exploring this new popular notion has happened: You ended up being on the wrong side of truth. It's a terrible thing to be wrong. But it's the fear of being wrong that makes us open the door to rumors.

A Dark Age

Imagine a time where there was no Internet, no cell phones, and no TiVo. Okay, so that was just the 1980s, a decade many of us love and some of us still live in. Test: Still holding on to "Where the Streets Have No Name" as the best rock anthem ever? Others of you are too young to remember life without an iPod. Test: Think that tight jeans and an old polyester vest over a T-shirt was your idea? Think again.

I digress.

Go back further in time. Before computers, before cars, before any kind of telephone, before electricity, before trains, before anyone you've ever talked to was born. Imagine a world before America, before democracy, before presidents and prime ministers, pastors and politicians. Imagine an age with no books in a language you could read.

Imagine you and your friends as farmhands working land neither you nor your fathers owned. Imagine a world only as big as what you could see on foot or by horseback. Any knowledge of a world beyond that came from the few brave souls who traveled by sea and were lucky enough to make it back alive

Imagine going to church and not understanding a word of what was being said—literally. Nothing. Not a single word. Imagine not owning a Bible, not even having access to one to read. Imagine not being able to read. The gigantic pictures on the colored windows, the ornate furnishings and massive stone structure, the elaborate robes, and all the choreographed movements and traditions were intended to help you understand God, to see His majesty and know His love. But instead, they make you feel small. And clueless. In the dark.

You would be living in the early medieval period, a time we have retrospectively and controversially dubbed "The Dark Ages." I have a bright young friend who earned his master of divinity and is currently working on his doctorate. He teaches at New Life School of Worship and has a gift for making dull history come alive for those born in the 1980s. He compares the Middle Ages to a really long camping trip. After enough time without soap and running water, people start acting a little strange. All of a sudden, hot dogs straight out of the packet sound like a gourmet meal; a rock is a down feather pillow; every sound of crunching leaves is a grizzly waiting to pounce.

Okay, so the analogy is a little bizarre. But the image is useful: People left in the dark without any access to information or the world beyond are prone to fear, superstition, and irrational decision making. And they make easy targets for the few who are in the know. Such were the life and times of the early Middle Ages.

There was only one church, one denomination of Christianity in the Western world. If you believed in God, and most would have acknowledged some measure of His existence, you were part of this church. But only the leaders of the church understood Latin, the language of the Scriptures and of the services. Only the church's insiders had access to records of important decisions on a variety of issues and interpretations of Scripture. For the common person, his knowledge of God was dependent on what his priest told him. And his priest's knowledge of God was largely dependent on what the pope and various councils told him.

And so the rumors spread. Rumors of how to please God, what things to say to God, what would make God act on your behalf—these were all people had. By the end of the Middle Ages, we find the church trying to sell poor peasants a piece of paper that would somehow grant a loved one passage from purgatory to paradise. Rumors. Crumbs. Oh yeah, and the profit from the sales would fund the rebuilding of St. Peter's Basilica.

To call this era "The Dark Ages" is controversial because such a moniker takes a progressive view of history—it reflects the perspective of the historian who believes the present is superior and more evolved, and the past is primitive or "dark" by comparison. Consider that the people living in the Middle Ages didn't know they were in the dark. They wouldn't have said they were missing out. It was all they knew. To use an example from my lifetime, now that I have a cell phone, I don't know how I lived without one. But before there were any cell phones, I never thought I was missing anything. But this controversy belies the strangest truth of living in the dark: You don't know what you don't know.

Whether you believe a peasant from the Middle Ages was worse off or better off than we are because of the lack of technology or afflu-ence, the inescapable reality is that the people who had knowledge and access to the Scriptures and ecclesial documents—the powerful church leaders of the Middle Ages—used their knowledge to their advantage, often exploiting the poor and illiterate. What made Martin Luther's Reformation so powerful was not simply his conviction that we are justified by faith, but the resultant belief that every believer is a priest and therefore has individual access to God. Luther's translation of the Scriptures into common German was the first Bible in well over five hundred years that was in a language people actually spoke in the marketplace. French, Spanish, Czech, English, and Dutch translations soon followed. Thanks to the printing press, it was also the first time in history that copies of the Bible were available to the masses. When Luther wrote hymns to God that borrowed tunes from old pub songs, the German church finally had a service in which the people could be participants and not mere observers. The trend caught on and the wildfires of Reformation—and they were as damaging as fires in some cases—spread all across Europe. No longer did people have to take someone else's description of God or resign themselves to secondhand information about what He was like; they could read the Bible, pray, worship, and engage God firsthand. As hard as it may be for us to imagine, few before Luther believed that was even possible.

From the Horse's Mouth

It's easy to understand why the common person in the Middle Ages lived by rumors of God, but why do we still today, in this age of information and technology? When we have more Bibles in the average American home than people, why do we still rely on a guy on TV for our info about God?

Years ago, as I sat in a chapel service at the Christian college I attended, I heard a preacher say that God was like a Coke machine. If we put money in a Coke machine, we expect to get a Coke. So why should we expect any different when we give to God? Blessings of spiritual "Cokes" should rain down on us every time we give. What was more appalling than his words were the "amens" I heard from the crowd. Did people really believe this stuff? Another chapel speaker made the whole student body—and our dear faculty against their wishes and better judgment—stand up and chant "Money cometh to me now!" complete with hand motions to close the service. Again, the craziest part was watching students hoop and holler like they had just gotten a free car on *Oprah*. It was a sort of spiritual "You go, girl!" in the strangest sense.

How did we get here?

With enough time, people start to create shortcuts for everything. In a capitalist society, we can hire an expert in any field. Sadly, the journey of knowing God is not exempt. Actually hearing God, engaging Him, is hard, tedious work. Isn't there some God expert we can hire to do the heavy lifting for us? Jesus, knowing our tendency to look for CliffsNotes, warned:

> *Don't look for shortcuts to God. The market is flooded with surefire, easygoing formulas for a successful life that can be practiced in your spare time. Don't fall for that stuff, even though crowds of people do. The way to life—to God!—is vigorous and requires total attention. (Matt. 7:13–14 MSG)*

But total attention is hard to give. And unwillingness to give it is not a uniquely American problem. Actually, it's an ancient one. Despite an amazing history of God's calling and dramatic redemption, Israel didn't waste much time in looking for shortcuts to God.

At Mount Sinai, before He gave Moses the commandments, God invited the people He had just rescued from captivity in Egypt to come near. They refused in fear. *Moses, you go for us.* God was trying to communicate that the rules He was about to give them were a sign of covenant, of relationship with them. He would be their God and they would be His people. But they preferred a less direct approach, someone else to mediate, someone else to relay God's wishes.

Later, they begged and pleaded for a king. When the prophet rebuked their childish request, he reminded them of the unique invitation they had been given: God wanted to be their king, to rule over them directly. He warned of how humans in authority, especially authority that has some measure of divine right attached to it, tend to abuse it and mistreat the people under them. Still, Israel insisted. *Let there be another to rule over us. Give us a king!*

Time and time again, God has drawn people to follow, to sit and listen, to watch and wait, to know Him. And yet the would-be God-followers delay for some reason or another.

As have we. We have preferred another to be our priest, our mediator, one who will tell us what God wants and what we must do in order to win His favor.

Maybe that's why some who wear the cloth of sacred office give in to these demands eventually. They know that they have no more claim to God-knowledge than you do, no more corner on the God-market than you have. But after enough Sundays and encounters with people who view them as God experts, they start obliging the expectation, believing the perception of who they are. It's not long before they start coining phrases, handing out formulas, and outlining steps to fix your marriage, get your business blessed, and make your kids icons of godliness.

Far too often, rumors about God originate in church. We hear a preacher say something about God with confident certainty, and we take it as truth. What we don't know is that he heard another preacher say it, and that preacher heard another preacher say it, and that preacher read it somewhere, and that author heard his momma say it, and so on.

We could blame them. But we would do better to blame ourselves for turning down God's invitation, for closing our ears and our eyes when He has tried to show Himself to us. No technological advancement, no access to information, no invention of convenience has been able to change the strange human impulse to shun God, to cover up and hide, the way the first man and woman did.

As a result we find ourselves so often wrong in ways big and small about God's nature, God's interests, God's reasons, and God's priorities. We are quickly fooled by clever rhymes and cultural truisms. To make it worse, we tell our wrongheaded notions to others in our everyday path. And so the rumors grow. Our unknowing, misguided God-perceptions sound truer each time we tell them. Soon enough, as rumors do, the notions that came from us work their way back to us from the lips of others. This is when we know they must be true. A circular trail of rumors can become verifiable truth, a community's dogma, in less than a generation.

If you believe it, you can receive it.

God knows your heart.

God just wants you to be happy.

It sounds right. People we respect say it, people who know a lot more than we do. And we don't want to miss out on something that might be true. We've heard it for so long, nobody has stopped to ask if it's true or why we think it might be.

There is a way that God designed us to encounter Him: firsthand. God has always preferred and invited firsthand communication. He desires to show Himself to us, speak to us, draw us to Himself. It is we humans, the objects of His affection, who have repeatedly declined.

God In a Box

It's an incredible irony that the only physical object the Israelites were allowed to use to represent their great, invisible, one true God was … a wooden box. Granted, it was overlain with gold and housed some very significant items. But still, at its core, it was a large wooden box.

This box, called the ark of the covenant (not to be confused with the giant boat Noah built) was the most sacred piece of furniture in Jewish life. Shortly after they were freed from slavery, the children of Israel were given instructions on how to worship the God who had delivered them. God gave them specifications for a large tent with three chambers. Each section had accompanying items and rituals that represented the sacrifice and sacredness of the approach to God. In the third and holiest chamber, there was only one item: the ark of the covenant. Only the high priest was allowed in, and even he only once a year, and even then with no guarantee of his survival.

The ark of the covenant was the thing the priests carried as they led the way across the Jordan River into the Promised Land. As they carried it, the waters of the mighty river at flood season parted. This ark was what the priests carried around Jericho as the walls came tumbling down.

These stories of the great miracles that came from God's presence in human situations have been an incredible source of inspiration to believers throughout the ages. I have often heard people in Christian circles say that all we need is the presence of God. "If only God would show up, then …" Fill in the dot-dot-dots: Our church would grow. Our problems would fade. Our business would be saved. The sick would be healed. Yet so many times, God is on the scene and life has gotten worse. He has been there, but nothing has changed—at least not in the way we hoped.

You see, there are other stories about the ark of the covenant, ones we talk less about. There came a time in Israel's history when the God whose presence on earth was represented by a box came to be treated as a sort of God-in-a-box who would pop up onto the scene

of trouble and make everything better. When life was going well,
God was ignored. Idols were worshipped. The ark was added to a list
of sacred items. In return, God's voice was not heard and His favor
was not known. This was Israel's version of the Dark Ages. During
those dim days, some strange and remarkable things occurred, all
involving the ark of the covenant. God's presence was repeatedly on
location, and yet horrid things took place. Lives were lost. Disease
struck. Tragedy permeated. Doubt, disappointment, sorrow. How
can God keep company with such dark emotions?

In the chapters that follow, we will take a closer look at each
tragic story involving the ark and uncover the rumors—the untrue
but popular notions—about God. These are not the only rumors
that are around today. I have chosen four that surface through these
stories and that are particularly relevant to our age. But there are
more. And my hope is that on each of our own journeys encoun-
tering God through Scripture and through His Spirit, a few more
rumors will be exposed in our hearts. Note that hidden in each story
of the ark is not only a rumor, but also a question, a question that
I believe, if followed to its end, will lead us to Christ. Through the
rumors and the questions we will discover what God might have
been trying to reveal about Himself. The things we uncover will give
us an opportunity to come near, to find a God we may not have
known. The risk is great, but the alternative is worse. For if we refuse
His invitation, we will find ourselves living in a new Dark Age, one
not dark by comparison to what comes after, but dark in the light of
Scripture's truth about who God is.

God's presence on the scene is not the end of the story, the time
to breathe a sigh of relief because God has arrived. God's presence on

the scene is only the beginning of a journey. After all, life with God is not just about God's arrival but also about our approach. The message of the misadventures of the ark of the covenant is simply this: We need more than God's presence; we need to learn how to see Him and respond to Him, how to engage Him in firsthand contact.

In the beginning God. This is how His story begins—with God speaking into the shapeless, vast cosmos, bringing order, meaning, and life. It is also how our story begins—with God on the scene, in the middle of our empty chaos, our "what the heck?" moment, speaking. He is inviting us on a journey, a long, narrow road of mystery and breathless wonder where rumors die and revelation comes alive.

DISCUSSION QUESTIONS:

1. Have you ever made a decision based on hearsay or a trend? What are some examples?

2. Have you preferred others to speak to God for you or tell you what God is like?

3. Do you expect that God's presence on the scene will solve everything?

3. Genie

Rumor #1: God Will Give Me What I Want.

Before I signed a mountain of papers and committed myself to a loan that would span more decades than I had been alive, I promised my father-in-law that Holly and I would be able to pay the mortgage on our new home from my income alone. He never asked; I just knew he would prefer it that way. And so did we. At the time, Holly was already quite pregnant with our first child, and none of us wanted her to be pressured into working—especially her. I never for a moment doubted that I could fulfill my promise. To be totally honest, I was a little annoyed that it might even be a question. Didn't he know my talent? Wasn't he aware of my job, the church I worked for, our ever-growing influence, our spiritual empire upon which the sun would never set?

I now understand his apprehension was not prompted by questions about my ability. Rather, his concern came from his knowledge of the volatility of life itself. He had lived long enough to understand that few things go as planned. As a farmer, he is reminded of this truth every day. As sophisticated as irrigation systems have become, people in Iowa still talk about rainfall. It matters. And it's as out of a farmer's control today as it was for farmers thousands of years ago. Soil and rain and bugs and so many other things—a bull's potency, a heifer's fertility, a chicken's durability—still determine a good year or a bad year. Even beyond nature, there are factors outside a farmer's control—the price of beef or poultry, the spike in cornfields as ethanol plants become big business. Few things go as planned. Much of life is beyond his control. He understands that. He is older, wiser.

I did not. I am younger and not-so-wise. I had always said that I would live in Colorado forever, keep doing what I was doing until I died. I thought I was being committed. I secretly and smugly congratulated myself for having mastered the art of staying steady. Now I wonder if my answers, dripping with certainty, came from a soul oblivious to uncertainty. I was so anesthetized by comfort, I hadn't noticed how I loved being in control, how I enjoyed and even expected life to go according to plan—if not in the details, then at least in the outcomes.

In the weeks and months that followed that Thursday, I felt like I was floating on a boat—not the kind where you go gently down the stream singing how life is but a dream—but the kind that feels like Pi Patel's in *The Life of Pi*, a raft in the middle of the mighty ocean, dark and ominous, vast and unpredictable. Would I have a job two months from now? What was my fallback plan? I couldn't believe this was happening. We could sell the house and move to the farm. There, at the very least, we could live off corn and eggs.

Still trying to plan, still grasping for control, still younger, not wiser. I began to understand that for all the gadgets and gizmos and digital attempts to capitalize on opportunity, increase efficiency, and predict my outcomes, I was still woefully out of control. I had planned, but I had not planned on this.

Surprised in the Suburbs

In my neighborhood, you can count on lawns looking uniform in their rock and grass outfits. You can spot your shutter colors on a house three doors down, but never right next door. You know the time the school bus arrives, the day the trash truck comes, and the week to set out your recycling items. There is even a precise moment, when the snow has stopped and the sun barely peeks through, that my neighbors, as if on cue, come out to shovel their driveways. I resist that last neighborhood norm, not because I march to the beat of a different drum but because I'm dreadfully cold all winter and would rather never stand outside at all. In every other way, I am just like my neighbors. I plan my vacations, pay my bills online, and obsess about my yard. As soon as my wife returns home from Target's after-Christmas sales, we're sitting in the kitchen planning how and with whom we'll spend next year's holidays. Even our gift giving is scripted. There is hardly an occasion where a person hasn't already registered for the things they want. You see, *surprise* is not in the vocabulary of the suburbs. We have a plan for everything.

It's no surprise, then, that our approach to church is quite the same. We want our services to start and end at precisely the same time every week. We want the same orderly flow of events within the service week after week. I mean, what would visitors think if all of a sudden we sang six songs instead of four? Even announcements must be planned weeks in advance so that the printed bulletin and the cooler-than-commercials videos align. After all, nobody wants to hear rambling live announcements from an awkward platform guy. There should be no surprises on Sundays.

Our sermons in suburbia are also fit to order. Three steps to lasting peace. Five ways to affair-proof your marriage. One simple secret to financial bliss. Six keys to raising brilliant kids. What a tremendous service to the community! All your problems solved, your messes cleaned up, your success guaranteed—in a sermon that's shorter than your favorite sitcom. What a deal! Could I get that with fries on the side?

And then something unexpected happens, something terrible. Only tragedy truly surprises in our neat worlds.[1] Nobody plans on losing their job. Or getting ill. Or having to sell their house. Tragedy is tragic because we wouldn't have chosen it, and we cannot control it. Tragedy is a reminder that the suburban life is not universal. What we have in common as human beings is not our drive for success; it's our experience of suffering. There are many things that lift Americans comfortably above the rest of the world. We spend more on lattes in a month than many people around the world earn in a year. But tragedy is the great equalizer. It reminds us that no matter how rich, how comfortable, how powerful, how successful we are—or how big our SUVs are—we are, at our core, fragile. We are vulnerable. There are things beyond our control. And, if we're honest, we don't like it.

When God Doesn't Follow the Plan

God's people, Israel of old, found themselves in difficulty time and time again. They were a small nation with many enemies, and so they were frequently in situations beyond their control. On one particular occasion, with their backs against the wall, they turned to a plan that had worked in battle before, one they were sure would work again.

It was in the days just before Samuel came of age as prophet and judge. Eli presided as priest, though his insight was failing and his courage was nonexistent. Israel was losing badly to their hated nemesis the Philistines. There was no choice. It was time to bring out their secret weapon: the ark of the covenant.

Never mind that they had been living with compromise, incorporating lewd pagan elements into the worship of the most holy God. Eli was too passive to either notice or care. He was out of touch with God and had lost the ability to make the people aware of the gravity of their sin. His own sons were desecrating the temple and exploiting worshippers. To make matters worse, the word of God had not been heard in a long time, and when a voice spoke to a young boy named Samuel, it was a word of judgment on Eli and his house, the religious establishment of the day.

But this was an emergency. Surely God would come through for them. It had worked before. It sounded like a good plan. Even the Philistines trembled when the ark was brought out onto the battlefield. That had to be a good sign.

Then the unthinkable happened. The Philistines rallied in the ninth and sent the Israelites home. Thousands died. Treasures were lost. The ark itself was captured. The beloved, sacred symbol of God's presence was taken by their foe, added to some collection of meaningless relics. Not only had they suffered a deathly blow to their nation's independence, but their only hope for salvation and restoration—God's presence—had been captured. To add to it, Eli and his two wicked sons had died—the sons in battle and Eli from hearing the news. Eli's grandson, born on that ominous day, was given the name "Ichabod"—"the glory is gone," or "woe to the glory of Israel." The good days were over.

In this story of the first misadventure of the ark of the covenant, we find a rumor about God exposed, a rumor that had grown in the absence of hearing God's voice. It is the first rumor for our journey: God Will Give Me What I Want.

In days void of vision and revelation, the people had begun to believe that God was their national genie, a sort of talisman to their own ends. The ark had been reduced to a lucky charm that would make troubles disappear and return life to halcyon days. Instead, this day ended in defeat and death, with God and His presence nowhere to be found. Tragedy had struck. Entirely unexpected. As it is with us, so it was for them.

Surprise is an emotion designed to make us take notice. It "jolts us to attention."[2] When some unexpected trouble comes, we are surprised and suddenly very alert. Even our physical response readies us to "listen." Chip and Dan Heath, in their brilliantly engaging book *Made To Stick*, describe our surprised expression:

When our brows go up, it widens our eyes and gives us a broader
field of vision—the surprise brow is our body's way of forcing us
to see more.... By way of contrast, when we're angry our eyes
narrow so that we can focus on a known problem. In addition
to making our eyebrows rise, surprise causes our jaws to drop
and our mouths to gape. We're struck momentarily speechless.
Our bodies temporarily stop moving and our muscles go slack.
It's as though our bodies want to ensure that we're not talking or
moving when we ought to be taking in new information.[3]

Surprise makes us see things we haven't seen before. For Israel, this was a battle they fully expected to win. Startled by the humiliating defeat, their eyes were opened. God had their attention. Psalm 78, a long account of Israel's history in the form of a song, describes God's version of this story:

But they put God to the test and rebelled against the Most
High; they did not keep his statutes. Like their fathers they
were disloyal and faithless, as unreliable as a faulty bow. They
angered him with their high places; they aroused his jealousy
with their idols. When God heard them, he was very angry;
he rejected Israel completely. He abandoned the tabernacle of
Shiloh, the tent he had set up among men. He sent the ark
of his might into captivity, his splendor into the hands of the
enemy. (Ps. 78:56–61)

The Philistines hadn't captured the ark; God sent it into their hands. By sending the ark into captivity, God was jolting Israel to

attention. After a long silence, He was speaking again on this catastrophic day, a day when Israel's spiritual jaws had hit the floor and
their eyes and ears were forced open. Their souls held captive, the
message hit them with full force, a message that still reverberates
today: *"I AM not here to do your bidding; you are here to do Mine."*

As You Wish

If you were a relative newcomer to church, you might be hard-
pressed to hear this same message. Everything about our invitation
to come to God is oriented around our needs. Are you down? Come
to Jesus, He'll make you happy. Are you broke? Start tithing and
God will make you rich. Think your life is meaningless and empty?
Come to Christ, and He'll lead you on a bravehearted adventure
so wild that William Wallace would be jealous. Every product created has to answer a crucial question before it is unleashed in the
Christian retail market: What is the felt need? How will this book
or CD or seminar or conference meet what people think they need?
Far too many church attendees are not disciples-in-the-making; we
are customers who are always right, consumers who need to have our
demands met. *What programs do you offer for my kids? What kinds of
conferences will you host to help my marriage? How do I know if I will
be fed here?* We've trained people to ask these questions because we've
insisted on answering them. Like a parent who enables his whining
child by constantly giving in, we've reinforced the worst impulses of
our consumer culture by turning church into a trade show, complete
with ads and exhibits for the latest, greatest program, conference, or
activity that will make them happier, healthier, and more successful.

Am I suggesting that God is not interested in our needs? Not at all. In fact, one of the things that distinguishes the God of the Bible from other deities is His profound interest in our lives. As Philip Yancey points out, while the ancient pagans believed that the actions of the gods spilled over into earth—e.g., when a god cries, it rains, etc.—the God of Israel repeatedly demonstrated how the actions of His people on earth deeply moved the God of heaven. When they prayed, He listened; when they called, He answered; when they obeyed, He blessed, protected, and defended; when they disobeyed, He disciplined them.[4]

But this interest, this compassion, this stooping to hear and act on behalf of humans has often been misread. We've taken God's love to mean His subservience to us. He becomes our cosmic errand boy, our Wesley in *The Princess Bride:* "As you wish." From the language and approach the church has employed, we are left to conclude that if the church—God's agent on earth—exists to cater to our every whim, then surely God must operate the same way.

We carry on in this state of sweet spiritual bliss until the unthinkable happens: Instead of the promotion, there is downsizing; instead of health, there is disease; instead of a wise investment home, it's a suffocating mortgage with evaporating equity.

What the heck? God! What happened to my wonderful life? Aren't You good?

That's when the realization starts to hit us: Something is wrong. There is a discrepancy between our view of God and our experience of life. Our God-concept is so thin it can't handle the weight of unexpected trouble.

At this point, many turn away. Bitter, hurt, confused, they walk away from their faith and dismiss God as the product of a foolish childhood imagination. Many never come back, ever. I suspect that even the most intelligent and obnoxious atheist doesn't have an intellectual problem with God; he has an experiential one. He has some story of how the life of someone he loved was not spared. His paradigm was shattered, his heart was broken, and so his mind went to work, dispelling and disproving the existence of an all-powerful, all-loving God.

But taking your toys and going home is not the only option; there is another way. It is more difficult, more messy, and entirely more uncomfortable. It is the approach the Jewish people, the ones God chose so long ago, decided to take. It is to wrestle with God. If there is any people group that should have walked away from God, it is the Jews. From Abraham's earliest descendants who suffered as slaves in Egypt to the fractured kingdoms of Israel and Judah, suffering is inextricably woven throughout the fabric of Jewish history. At the hand of the Assyrians, ten tribes were scattered and lost; under the Babylonians, the other two were taken into exile. The Romans distrusted them, the Byzantines ostracized them, the Muslims persecuted them, and many in the name of Christ sought to destroy them. As if the first five thousand or so years of their history were not dark enough, the last century bears the stain of the horrific events of the Holocaust. Yet the Jewish faith has survived. It has not been eradicated from history. It remains among the oldest religions—if not *the* oldest religion—of the world. Why have so many orthodox Jews, the people experiencing such incredible suffering and turmoil, not abandoned their faith or dismissed God as a hoax or a fairy tale?

I suspect it is because they have learned to wrestle with God. After all, as one writer friend noted to me the other night, was not

Jacob's name changed to "Israel" precisely because of his struggle with God? Elie Wiesel, a Holocaust survivor, wrote bluntly about his experience: "I rarely speak about God. To God, yes. I protest against Him. I shout at Him. But to open a discourse about the qualities of God, about the problems that God imposes, theodicy [the problem of a good, powerful God and the existence of pain, evil, and suffering], no. And yet He is there, in silence, in filigree."[5]

You can't wrestle from a distance. It is a full-contact sport that places you in uncomfortably close proximity to another. Wrestling with God allows us to see Him more clearly and more correctly. And perhaps, more completely.

An Incomplete Picture

My wife relayed a story of a pastor's wife sharing a "praise report" with the other ladies at a prayer meeting. She had gone shopping that weekend and was so grateful the Lord had granted her a parking spot close to the mall. Wow, isn't God good? He ignores mass genocide in Rwanda, but cares enough to get you closer to JCPenney. We are messed up in our heads. When did we start believing that we are the center of the universe, that God Himself lives for our pleasure and comfort? It's one thing to give God credit for all the good in your life. I'm all for thanking God for raises and good test scores. But to take that extra step, to somehow believe that He owes us as much, that divine mollycoddling is God's favorite pastime, is nothing short of egocentric lunacy.

Another woman who had recently moved to Colorado told me how certain she was that God was going to give her and her husband the house of their dreams because of all they had sacrificed. He might. God is loving and lavish. But it seems like such thinking is missing the point. It is incomplete at best.

I hear you protest: "Your unexpected difficulties came because of someone's sin. Israel's tragic day stemmed from their disobedience."

True.

"If I live in obedience," you continue, "my life will be just fine. I will be blessed."

Maybe.

Or maybe you're missing the deeper matter. My point is simply this: There are things in life beyond our control. And God is first among them. God will not tolerate being used as an instrument to control our own lives. Obedience is not a sort of magic code, an "Abracadabra" that moves God to action—or worse, forces Him to action. If we tithe, if we pray, if we confess, if we believe, then our businesses will grow, our children will flourish, and everything we touch will turn to gold. I know of churches that, as they give their tithes and offerings, recite something to this effect: "With this offering I sow my seed and I expect a harvest. I call forth raises, bonuses, promotions, ideas, and money due me."

I struggle with these depictions of God. I am uncomfortable around people who talk so smugly about God's blessings, as though they were inevitable. As if because of their obedience God was bound to act in their favor, like a genie who had been released from his lamp and now owed his liberator three wishes. People who think this way point to all the "if ... then" clauses in the Old Testament. Deuteronomy 28 is among the favorite passages.

If you fully obey the LORD your God and carefully follow
all his commands I give you today, the LORD your God will
set you high above all the nations on earth. All these bless-
ings will come upon you and accompany you if you obey the
LORD your God: You will be blessed in the city and blessed
in the country. The fruit of your womb will be blessed, and
the crops of your land and the young of your livestock—the
calves of your herds and the lambs of your flocks. Your basket
and your kneading trough will be blessed. You will be blessed
when you come in and blessed when you go out. The LORD
will grant that the enemies who rise up against you will be
defeated before you. They will come at you from one direction
but flee from you in seven. The LORD will send a blessing
on your barns and on everything you put your hand to. The
LORD your God will bless you in the land he is giving you.
(Deut. 28:1–8)

Obedience will be met with prosperity and protection; disobedience will be chastened with pain and hardship. If only life were
that clean and simple. One needs only to keep reading in the Bible
to find out that is not the case.

I have heard some say that God blesses American Christians
with close parking spaces and cable TV because of our nation's history of godliness. Every time I hear it, I have to swallow the vomit
in the back of my mouth. How do we account for the fact that
the regions of the world that are experiencing the most aggres-
sive growth in Christianity—Africa, Latin America, and Asia (the
"Global South")—are also places riddled by poverty and disease?[6]

But besides the massive quagmire of trying to assess which nation has been more "godly" and therefore deserves more Twinkies, I'm not sure God sees us in terms of nation-states anyway. Wasn't that Jesus' point to the disciples who kept asking when He would restore the kingdom to Israel? The kingdom is not of this world. And neither are its best benefits.

The larger problem is that we have selective listening and learning when it comes to God's Word. We memorize Psalm 23 because of its promise that we "shall not want," while we ignore Psalm 22 and its fist-against-the-ground-you-never-hear-me-when-I-pray complaints. Both are written by David, and, for crying out loud, they're side by side. We want to believe in the God who always leads us to still waters and never in the God who seems to have forsaken us. We want the God of green pastures and not the one who is silent in our suffering. But He is both. And until we accept Him as God of both we haven't accepted Him as God at all. We have only been following a genie, a doting godfather in the sky who whimsically dispenses goodies to some of His kids while ignoring others for no rhyme or reason.

I cannot answer why some suffer while others do not. I understand that the dynamics of free will and a fallen world play some role. But still, why God intervenes some times and chooses not to at others is a mystery. I believe that, in the end, redemption—God's ability to take what was lost or messed up and make it work for our good and His glory—is more powerful than prevention or intervention. I believe that future glory far outweighs momentary afflictions. But why the momentary afflictions, why the trouble in this world that is allowed to persist? God only knows. And that is the point: There are some things only God knows and understands. To deny as much is to have reduced God into our image.

God is not a Coke machine. He resists formulas and equations, even the ones He apparently gave. To fully get this picture of a wildly personal, living God, you cannot just read Deuteronomy 28; you have to also wrestle with the psalmists, lament with Jeremiah, protest with Jonah, and weep with the Son of God Himself. To string together our favorite list of verses containing "God's promises for the blessed life" is like living in voluntary ignorance, a Dark Ages by choice. It is simply immature and foolish.

It is also surprisingly modern. That wasn't how a Jew treated his own covenant and Scriptures. The Hebrew word used for God's love for His people is the word *hesed.* It's hard for Old Testament scholars to define this word in English. Vine's Expository Dictionary suggests it is a combination of strength, steadfastness, and love.[7]

Hesed is played out in the dramatic love story of Hosea and his adulterous wife, Gomer. Through Hosea's living metaphor, God declares his own unfailing love to Israel, his wayward bride. "I will betroth you to me forever," God said to Israel. "I will betroth you in righteousness and justice, in *love* and compassion. I will betroth you in faithfulness, and you will acknowledge the LORD" (Hos. 2:19–20).

Moses uses this word as he describes God's covenant to Israel in Deuteronomy, a sort of preface to the specifics that follow some twenty chapters later: "Know therefore that the LORD your God is God; he is the faithful God, keeping his covenant of love to a thousand generations of those who love him and keep his commands" (Deut. 7:9).

But the most amazing thing about *hesed* is the light it sheds on God's covenant with His people. *Hesed* often implies a relationship between a stronger party and a weaker party, where the weaker party seeks protection and blessing from the stronger but cannot claim it as a right. The stronger party keeps his promise out of *hesed* though he has the freedom to implement it the way he chooses. Still, the *hesed* on the part of the stronger party shows great generosity, loyalty, and mercy.[8] To the Jew, God kept His covenant with them out of His unswerving covenantal love—not out of a sense of obligation or debt. So a Jew would likely never make the kinds of outrageous "you owe me" claims that many modern Christians do of God. Covenant is not a bargaining chip.

The richness of covenant was reinforced in Jewish minds at an early age. A young Jewish boy in Jesus' day had to memorize the Torah by the time he was ten. They would have been well-versed not only in the blessings and curses associated with the covenant, but also in the dilemmas. Why was Abel, the one whose offering was pleasing and acceptable to God, not protected from his murderous, jealous brother? Why did Joseph, the favored son, suffer so much abuse? Why was Moses, by far the most faithful and obedient of his generation, kept out of the Promised Land despite his patient leadership of a pack of grumblers and complainers? As if that were not enough, between the ages of ten and fourteen, a Jewish boy coming of age would then learn to answer questions with more questions, showing that he had identified the many dilemmas of life with God. It's also at this age that he would memorize the Psalms, the Prophets, and much of the rest of the Old Testament. Memorized. Stories, complaints, laments, blessings, curses, perplexing issues—all hidden in the heart. What would it do to our picture of God if we even *read* the Old Testament, let alone attempted to commit it to memory? It is true, we see in part while on this side of heaven. But we see even less when we pick and choose our favorite verses and stories of Scripture while ignoring the rest.

Friends, this cannot be. We've got to listen to the whole counsel of Scripture and let it widen our view and open our hearts. It will lead us to wrestle with God as Jacob did, all through the dark night of our soul, and help us emerge in the daylight with a new name, having seen God face-to-face.

DISCUSSION QUESTIONS:

1. Has God ever surprised you by not acting the way you expected?

2. Have you ever thought that God "owes" you something because of your obedience?

3. What do you do when God doesn't seem to follow the plan? How do you wrestle with Him?

4. Gone

Question #1: Where Has the Glory Gone?

When the National Weather Center downgraded Hurricane Katrina from a Category 5 to a Category 3, those who remained in New Orleans probably believed the worst was over. There was damage from wind and rain, but it certainly didn't have the mark of the "big one." There were probably many reasons that people stayed in New Orleans that August weekend in 2005. Some might have been hardened cynics, refusing to believe the severity of the storm; others might have been unwilling to sit in hours of traffic or deal with the enormous inconvenience of evacuation. Many were stuck with few options and not enough time.

Janice Mahaney had the stomach flu and didn't feel like spending sixteen hours in a car. Despite the persistent pleadings of friends, Janice refused to evacuate. When her close friend and roommate called hours later to check on her, she reported that damage was bad, but it didn't seem catastrophic. "Everything's fine."

She could not have guessed what would happen next.

Within hours after the downgraded hurricane had passed, New Orleans was underwater.

A 10-foot storm surge whipped up by high winds had blown in off Lake Pontchartrain, traversed the London Avenue Canal and caused a 60-foot breach in its wall. Eventually, the 11-mile-long east-west residential corridor surrounding Lakefront/Gentilly [where Janice lived] was under 6 to 12 feet of water. It was one of 50 breaches that caused the flooding of 80 percent of New Orleans, a 120-square-mile area.[1]

It was already dark by the time the water started rising in Janice Mahaney's home. Wading in a chest-high current, she watched as lizards and snakes darted toward the ceiling. In the chaos of the moment, her own home seemed strangely unfamiliar. Finally she made her way outside, where a sofa cushion became her flotation device. Unable to reach a rooftop, Janice bobbed in the water for sixteen hours—all through the night—waiting for rescue. Helicopters flew overhead, taking in the mangled city scene but oblivious to the individual fighting for her life. At last a neighbor came by in a boat and shuttled her to a nearby school where help finally came.

In an interview with *Reader's Digest* about a year after Katrina, Janice Mahaney talked about that harrowing night in New Orleans and about all she had lost in the storm. At the time of the interview, she was unemployed, suffering "night terrors, exhaustion, memory loss, and post-traumatic stress" and battling a lingering illness with mysterious symptoms—which she believes resulted from floating in putrid water for so long.[2]

Many citizens of New Orleans talk about the homes, the memorabilia, or the property they lost. For Janice Mahaney, a piece of her soul was washed away that night, gone forever.

Losing God

What do you notice in tragedy's wake?

What is it that you miss the most?

As a pastor, I've watched believers walk through the most unimaginable tragedies. I've talked almost every week over the last few months with the father who lost two daughters in the tragic shooting that happened at New Life Church barely a year after the scandal. His heart is broken. But through sorrow and intense grief, there is still some faint light in his heart. It is the light of hope. Like a small floating cushion in the murky floodwaters of sorrow, he and his family cling to God with all they have inside. For them, as with so many other believers who have suffered loss, there is the sense that though they have lost so much, they have not lost God, and therefore have not ultimately lost hope.

A team of students from the New Life School of Worship recently returned from two weeks in Uganda, loving and serving orphans. An incredible indigenous ministry called Christian Life Ministries built over seventy orphan homes in two villages. In one of the villages, the children and their house moms would come out into the compound's common area every evening and burst in spontaneous rhythms and songs of praise. From the stories I heard, it sounded like a scene of epic beauty.

Matt Vogel, one of the team leaders, still in his early twenties, summed up what hit him hardest: "These people embody the belief that even when you've lost everything, God is enough." They prayed, they worshipped, they laughed and loved like God was enough for them. In the face of devastating loss and seemingly insurmountable odds, they had hope because they had God.

But how would it be if you had lost God?

How must it have felt for Israel on the day that they lost the ark of the covenant? Not only had they lost friends and fathers, sons and brothers, not only had they lost their leader and sense of certainty and security, they had lost God. Out of the ashes of that devastating day came a question that haunted their nation for years to come: "Where has the glory gone?"

Eli's daughter-in-law, the wife of Phinehas, was pregnant and near her time of delivery. When she heard that the Ark of God had been captured and that her father-in-law and husband were dead, she went into labor and gave birth. She died in childbirth, but before she passed away the midwives tried to encourage her. "Don't be afraid," they said. "You have a baby boy!" But she did not answer or pay attention to them. She named the child Ichabod (which means "Where is the glory?"), for she said, "Israel's glory is gone." She named him this because the Ark of God had been captured and because her father-in-law and husband were dead. Then she said, "The

*glory has departed from Israel, for the Ark of God has been
captured." (1 Sam. 4:19–22 NLT)*

Of all that had been lost that day—thousands of lives, their
priest and only leader, their dignity, their security—the loss that left
the most gaping hole was the loss of God's presence, the absence of
God's glory. Even a mother in the midst of childbirth knew it.

The loss that mattered most, the one they wept most bitterly
about, the one that made that day go down in history as one of
Israel's darkest days was the loss of God's presence. On a day when
everything had been taken away, they suddenly realized the only
thing worth having above all else: God.

Not a token, not a trinket, not a charm. God. The living, active,
personal presence of God. Their God, the One who had rescued
them from Egypt, led them through the wilderness, and brought them
into the Promised Land. The God of Abraham, Isaac, and Jacob.
Not just some god, some deity, or legend. Not the generic kind or
the pluralistic kind. Not the one about whom little was known, the
vague, capricious, mythological god. No. It was the God who had
broken into time and space. The God who spoke at Sinai and gave
the Ten Commandments. The God who cared, the God who had
chosen them. Their God, the God of Israel.

He was gone.

Don't Know What You've Got

It was the fall of 1997 when I met Holly Michael. She was eighteen
and full of sunshine. Her blonde hair glistened in the Oklahoma sun,

and I didn't think I could find the courage to meet her blue eyes. I was looking through a pair of gold-rimmed, oval-shaped glasses and dressed in a blend of hand-me-downs and sales-rack steals. She looked like the quintessential American girl; I looked like the epitome of an international student.

A mutual friend introduced us, but neither of us thought much of that moment. It was about two months later that Holly and I really began to talk. It was a ballroom dancing birthday party for a friend. We had come with dates simply because the party required it, not because we were attached. Somehow, in the course of the night, we met, sans our dance partners, around the punch bowl. Her date preferred to find ways of doing the "YMCA" to polka music, and mine preferred sitting. So, after a few words of nervous conversation, we spent the rest of the party swing dancing together. Kind of. I'm a terrible dancer. But there was something about holding her hands in mine, something about the way she smiled, that made even our clumsy dance moves seem magical. That night a flame was lit, a connection in our hearts that would not easily be lost.

I wish I could say that from then on we marched unswervingly toward courtship and marriage, but that was not the case. I had a period of panic. And Holly, two years behind me in school, needed time before she was ready to make a lifelong commitment. Three years, to be exact. In retrospect, it was an incredible time of strengthening the bonds of our friendship. But the roller coaster of an on-again-off-again dating relationship was grueling for both of us. I was getting ready to move to Colorado, and it was time to either get on the marriage-bound train or say our good-byes.

Unfortunately, the summer of 2000 turned out to be the most miserable one of my life. I can still remember sitting on the couch telling Holly that I loved her and that I was so grateful to have had her in my life. I was a better man for having been with her, even if it was only destined to be for a season. She was sobbing. Everything inside told her she loved me, but she somehow wasn't able to give her whole heart to me … forever. After three years of friendship and love, it was time to concede that maybe this just wasn't meant to be. It was the strangest thing to feel such a strong connection to another person and yet have to let it go. That tearful July night, heavy with the mugginess of an Oklahoma summer and the weight of love lost, we said good-bye for good. A few weeks later, I loaded up my Jeep and headed for Colorado.

Holly will tell you that it wasn't until I left Oklahoma that summer that something became clear in her heart. For the first time, she got a taste of what life would be like without me. And she didn't like it. Doubt dissipated quickly. Her friends encouraged her to wait several months before making any contact with me.

Then came the e-mail—a short, simple "prayer request" sort of e-mail. But I knew it was more. I wanted it to be. I was hollow without her. I mean, I knew I loved her and I knew she was special. But I didn't think I would have such a hard time letting her go. So when the e-mail came in, I didn't reply. I called her. We ended up talking on the phone all night. That once slack and dusty connection that tethered our souls now pulled tight and strong.

Then, that beautiful day in October, she showed up in Colorado. It was fall break, and she and a few others had come to visit. I invited her to tag along with me while I ran a few errands for work. My main assignment that day was to find a sled for our Christmas production, and it required a trip up to a quaint mountain town. Well, as fate— or, ahem, the Lord—would have it, her car broke down right there in Green Mountain Falls, where the cool Colorado air was blowing and the leaves were proudly displaying their brilliant fall wardrobe. We found ourselves stuck waiting for a tow truck with plenty of time to talk. As the day went on, one thing became crystal clear: We did not want to live without each other. As fulfilling as my ministry job was, I was incomplete without her. As much as she desired to have it written in the sky, it was now undeniable in her heart. The time was now right. Love's time had come at long last. We were going to spend a lifetime confirming what we had suspected from the first dance: We were made for each other.

A few months later, Holly and I were on a plane bound for Malaysia. She had met my parents before, but it was time to spend some quality time with them. There, on a remote island resort, with the help of my sister, mother, and father, I asked her to be my wife. She said yes, and by summer's end, we were Mr. and Mrs. Packiam. (Kleenex, please.)

But it took our relationship being gone for us to get it back. It took living without each other, visualizing a future without the other in it, to lead us to the place of wholehearted love.

Don't it always seem to go that you don't know what you've got 'til it's gone.[3]

So it often is with God. We don't recognize the value of relationship with Him until He's gone. Not that He walks away; He promised He would never do that. God is "gone" from us the same way He was in Eli's day before the ark was actually taken away. In many ways, the loss of the ark of the covenant for Israel was just an outward sign of an inward spiritual loss that had occurred long ago. Israel had lost God when they stopped hearing His voice, when they ignored His commands and did "what was right in [their] own eyes" (Judg. 21:25 NKJV). Their attempt to pull God out of hiding and get Him to do their bidding was proof that they had been without God—the one, true, holy, awesome, loving, and terrifying God— long before that day.

For us, God is gone when we fail to see Him or seek Him. He is gone when we treat Him like a lucky charm, a thing to be stowed away in a dusty chest and pulled out only in a crisis. He is gone when we insist on letting someone else go to Him for us instead of going to Him ourselves. In all those ways and more, He is gone not because He actually left but because we never really let Him be present in our lives. I wonder if He then finds a way to make His absence felt, like a lover who will be taken for granted no more, just to give us enough pause to recognize what we've lost. After all, He loves it when we seek Him, search for Him. Seeking is what He sent His Son to earth to do for us while we were lost. And seeking is how He wants us to live, like a lover who can't live without the Beloved. Seeking just might be God's love language. But when we begin to ignore or avoid Him, when we lose the recognition of Him as God—sovereign and loving—He is gone.

And one day—whether from tragedy or from something unexpected or simply by God's mercy—we are jolted awake and ask that haunting question, "Where has the glory gone?"

A Lesser Blessing

That question is the beginning of our salvation. That question is the first sign that we have begun to realize that none of the things we have called blessings are enough to compare to what God calls "glory." Glory is eternal. It cannot be taken away. In its light, our present afflictions will seem slight and momentary. Glory is our destiny; it is what we will become and what we will enjoy forever. Glory is the invisible attributes of God being made visible, tangible—and enjoyable.

Yet on this earth, in this life, we are prone to keep clamoring for the lesser blessing.

> *We are half-hearted creatures, fooling about with drink and sex and ambition when infinite joy is offered us, like an ignorant child who wants to go on making mud pies in a slum because he cannot imagine what is meant by the offer of a holiday at the sea. We are far too easily pleased.*[4]

C. S. Lewis was talking about sin being the lesser pleasures. But it is true of all earth's pleasures, even the ones we count as blessings. We are quick to speak of how the new covenant is better than the old, and how thankful we are to be New Testament believers. But I wonder if we get it. If we think the new covenant is so much better, why do we keep praying for the blessings of the old? Paul, challenging the believers in Ephesus, reminds them that they are "blessed … with every spiritual blessing" (Eph. 1:3). What house or job or car could compete with that? We so easily forget Jesus' chastisement of those who seek to build bigger and bigger barns as if early blessing were God's reward. I am guilty of this. If the Son of God Himself told us to store up treasures in heaven, why do I keep looking for Him to fill my bank account?

In another of his works, C. S. Lewis describes how God often awakens us to the greater blessing He has for us through the unlikely instrument of pain. Lewis gently wrote, "God, who made these deserving people, may really be right when He thinks that their modest prosperity and the happiness of their children are not enough to make them blessed: that all this must fall from them in the end, and that if they have not learned to know Him they will be wretched."[5]

You see, there is a greater blessing we often miss. It's the blessing of knowing God, of growing in an active, living knowledge of Him. Jesus Himself is the Treasure in heaven. (Can bigger mansions—even celestial ones—or a larger estate on golden streets really compare to the glorious Son of God?) To know Him is to have eternal life.

Could it be that God might—maybe—allow the lesser blessings to be taken from our hands so that He might give us the greater ones? In our thickheadedness, we so easily and often choose the lesser blessings, often even at the expense of the greater ones. We sacrifice time with our kids to gain just a bit more money, or skip out on date nights with our spouse to go to one more meeting at church. We work to build God's kingdom while ignoring the incredible gift of friendship with the King Himself. Time and time again, without even thinking or blinking, we give up the best for all that is good. I suspect God operates differently.

I am not here to say that trouble or loss comes from God.

Personally, I don't believe that. Furthermore, whether trouble comes because of your sin, someone else's sin, or Adam's sin is irrelevant to our discussion. Trouble, regardless of its source, is a fact of life in a fallen world. Jesus said it plainly to His disciples: "In this world you will have trouble" (John 16:33). Parsing the source of our trouble is not the main thing because fixing it is not the main thing. If it were, Jesus would have gone on to tell His disciples the four reasons bad things happen to good people and how they could neatly avoid those situations. He could have identified the roots of trouble and taught them the mantras for making it go away.

Instead, Jesus goes on to say, "Take courage; I have overcome the world" (John 16:33 NASB). I doubt that He meant, "Don't worry. You can use me to control your outcomes, forecast your glowing futures, and avoid this trouble." A few chapters later, Jesus does indeed predict Peter's future—and it's not pleasant. If there was ever a group that would understand hope in the midst of trouble, it was the disciples. Over the course of their lives they would endure the most brutal persecution and the bitterest disappointments. Their hope was not in a special confession or formula that would make them rich or comfortable. Their hope was in the conviction that this world was not the only world. This trouble was not their final state. Suffering is not the last word. Because Christ overcame death itself, the last and final mortal trouble, there was hope for another world, a better country, a heavenly city. And the Treasure there—theirs and ours—is Christ.

The greatest blessing and the lesser blessings can coexist. In fact, often as Christians we find ourselves exclaiming, "All this, and heaven, too?" But only one comes with the chance of the other. If we fix our eyes on the blessing of knowing Christ, both now and in heaven forever, we may just find ourselves surprised by the lesser blessings of friendship, love, and family. And sometimes, the inferior gifts of houses and cars and jobs are part of our lot as well. But if we choose to occupy our hearts with the best of earth, we are doomed to miss the best there is: God Himself.

And God, in His love, will do everything He can to help us avoid that fatal mistake.

The Gift of Disappointment

Trouble often looks like an unmet expectation, a kind of deep disappointment that opens our eyes. It makes us ask if somehow, previously unbeknownst to us, we've been using God as just another gadget, the latest technological advance sure to make our lives easier and more efficient. Disappointment, after all, is an agent of the cross. It reminds us that we are not in control and that we were never meant to be. "The creature's illusion of self-sufficiency must, for the creature's sake, be shattered," Lewis wrote.[6] The disappointment that comes from an unexpected trouble, an unplanned difficulty, can help us die to ourselves, to our attempts at control, to our plans for the perfect life. Disappointment is an agent of the cross.

But it is also a means of resurrection. It comes as a gift to us, a gift of perspective. It awakens us to God and the richness of His life in us. It helps us, as St. Augustine suggested, to let go of the lesser gifts so that our hands are open to receive the Greatest Gift.[7]

The people of Israel, in the wake of the horrific loss of life and the missing presence of God, rediscovered obedience. Disappointment can open our eyes to all the ways we were hoping to be the one in charge. It can expose the secret places where the reins are tightly in our grip. Jesus is the Lord whom we confess, but disappointment can make Him the Lord whom we serve. We are led, often by the hand of trouble and disappointment in life, to the place of obedience and surrender. When life doesn't go according to our plan, we start to remember the One whose plans are never thwarted. What God establishes will never fail. The wisdom of the ancient Hebrews phrased it this way: "Many are the plans in a man's heart, but it is the LORD's purpose that prevails" (Prov. 19:21).

God is to be obeyed. But not for the blessings that might come in this life. God is to be obeyed because that is the proper response to an Almighty God. Obedience reminds us that we are the servants, He is the master. It's not a way to get God to do something for us. In fact, obedience isn't about getting anything; it's about giving everything. Obedience does indeed lead us to blessing—God Himself, the greatest blessing of all.

In the wake of the scandal that shook our church, I would lay in bed thinking about my different options, wondering if I would have any tomorrow. Slowly, the truth settled in my heart: It doesn't matter. It doesn't matter if I don't have a job tomorrow. It doesn't matter if we have to sell the house. I know God. I have Him and He has me. I began to realize that I didn't care what God did or wouldn't do for me. I stopped praying for Him to rescue our church or save this particular organization. I stopped because I realized I was praying out of fear of losing my livelihood rather than conviction in the purpose for our existence. I had a vested interest in our church not going under. The truth was, if our church folded, there were about five hundred others in town for people to choose from. It didn't matter if He gave me a sweet future on earth. I have a future in heaven where neither moth nor rust can cause decay. I know Him. And He knows me. I have glory. It is well, it is well with my soul.

DISCUSSION QUESTIONS:

1. Can you imagine life without God?

2. What greater blessings have you traded for lesser blessings?

3. How has disappointment been an agent of the cross in your life?

5. Many

Rumor #2: God Can Be Added to My List of Loyalties.

The tattoo on his left tricep simply reads "Get Rich to This." Sure, it was inspired by a Goodie Mob song he loved in college, but for Asante Samuel, the phrase has come to define him. Two Super Bowl rings are good and fine, but what really matters is money. For more money, he would ditch old teammates, throw chemistry and team goals by the wayside, and give up his best chance of winning another ring. In the spring of 2008, Asante Samuel made the decision to leave the history-making New England Patriots and sign with the ringless Philadelphia Eagles. In former teammate Wes Welker's words, Samuel "chose money over championships."[1]

But Asante Samuel is not alone. Every summer, NFL players start holding out of minicamps, demanding more money or a trade. At some point their agent—usually Drew Rosenhaus—ends up on TV explaining how $5 million a year is just simply not enough and as a matter of fact is quite insulting to an athlete in his twenties whose talent and stats demand a much higher salary. When asked to explain this kind of gall and greed, this phrase will inevitably turn up in every interview on TV and radio: It's a business.

It's a business that you only get to work in for ten years, and that long if you're lucky. So, you have to make in ten years what the rest of us hope to earn in forty. Except that the athletes usually involved in disputes are not the ones making a measly $200,000 a year; it's usually the ones who earn more in one year than what we could hope our IRA will be worth after thirty years of investing. Asante Samuel, for example, was unhappy with his previous one-year contract of $7.79 million. His new contract is worth $57 million over six years.

There's big money in the business of pro football, and players want a slice. It's understandable since they're the ones sacrificing their bodies week after week. But the thing I can't get over is how often the same players who are breaking their word, getting out of contracts, and grabbing as much money as they can are the same ones who "just wanna thank the Lord and Savior, Jesus Christ." They are more than willing to grab a mic and give God all the glory so long as they can get all the money. To be fair, I've never heard anything that remotely connects Asante Samuel to Christianity, so he's not the villain; he's acting on what he thinks is best. But since Samuel's story is not uncommon, sadly even among Christian athletes, it begs a host of larger questions, ones that are closer to home: Can greed and God coexist? Does God share our values of gaining more money?

At the core, we need to know, can God be added to a list of loyalties?

Can there be many things that have our allegiance, as long as God or religion is first among them?

When I was in high school, I realized that I had a "report card" view of life. The areas of my life were categories like classes that I needed to evaluate and grade myself on. There was my social life, my family life, my music life, my academic life, my sports and hobbies, and, of course, my spiritual life. Every now and then, as I had my devotional time with God, I would mentally check through the list and see how I was doing. *Pretty good in spiritual life. Give it an A. Not bad in school stuff. Probably a B+. Social life … hmm … I dunno, let's say a B.* Life is organized by priorities and goals, and God tops that list. Isn't that how it should be? What's wrong with that?

Meeting Dagon

After the Philistines defeated Israel and captured the ark of the covenant, they took the ark to their city, Ashdod, and placed it in Dagon's temple.

Dagon was an ancient god, regarded as chief among the pantheon of pagan gods. In the ancient city of Ebla, Dagon was the head over some two hundred deities, given the title "lord of the gods." Of all the gods they worshipped, Dagon was supreme. He was also known as "lord of the land." The Ugaritic root for his name—DGN—means "grain," as does the Hebrew version, Dagan. It's also possible that his name is connected to the Arabic "DAGN," which means "rain" or "rain cloud." The implication is that he was the god who allowed grains to flourish and rain to fall. Since grain and its success was inherent to the well-being of an ancient agrarian culture, Dagon was, in a way, the god who gave increase. In Akkadian inscriptions, Dagon is referred to as "a powerful and warlike protector."[2] He was the god who helped warriors conquer lands and expand their kingdoms.

You might surmise that Dagon was the god of increase and victory—in short, the god of success.

It is likely, then, that for the Philistines, the temple of Dagon was a house of idols, a collection of pagan deities among whom Dagon was supreme. Into that house they bring the sacred ark of the covenant, the symbol of Israel's invisible, all-powerful, redeeming God. It is not difficult to guess their motives for adding the God of Israel to their already-large collection of gods. They probably reasoned that as far as deities go, the more the merrier. If one god equaled peace, and another fertility, and Dagon was over all as the god of increase, victory, and success, then it seemed like they would have an unbeatable collection of gods by adding the famed God of Israel—the God who had destroyed the mighty Egyptians back in the day, the God who had helped a tiny, obscure family become a strong and stable nation. Maybe it was the first instance in history of a collector's impulse: *Gods of the Ancient World—Collect them all!* Or maybe it was a sort of Dream Team of deities, kind of like the USA Olympic men's basketball team with Magic Johnson, Larry Bird, *and* Michael Jordan. Together, these gods would form an unstoppable force, marching the Philistines inexorably toward world domination, crushing any that dared stand in the way. These thoughts might have danced in their heads that night as they set the ark of the covenant in the temple of Dagon.

But a funny thing happened the next morning.

They carried the Ark of God into the temple of Dagon and placed it beside an idol of Dagon. But when the citizens of Ashdod went to see it the next morning, Dagon had fallen with his face to the ground in front of the Ark of the LORD! So they took Dagon and put him in his place again. (1 Sam. 5:2–3 NLT)

The great Dagon had fallen in a worship posture before the presence of the God of Israel. This was a major "what the heck?" moment. Although, because they were Philistines, it was probably expressed in language more foul. This was not what they had in mind when they triumphantly marched into town with Israel's most sacred piece of furniture. They had conquered Israel and, so they thought, Israel's God. But now something was horribly wrong.

I imagine it was a PR nightmare for the priests of Dagon. I can imagine their frantic conversations early that morning.

Who saw this happen? Has he told anyone? No one can know that our great god Dagon has fallen prostrate before the God of Israel!

What? Some have already heard!

Okay … well, tell them it was a coincidence. After all, the winds were strong last night, and Dagon is a rather tall idol. There's no hidden meaning or message here. Just a fluke.

What's that? They'll never buy that!

I know. You're right. We're in trouble.

A Savvier Christianity

How often do we—consciously or unconsciously—bring God into a temple of Dagon? How often in our lives is Christ living among idols, specifically the idol of increase, victory, and success? You may protest, but the question we may never have bothered to ask ourselves is if our desire to serve Christ and our drive to succeed in life are mutually agreeable goals. By the preaching in many churches in America today, the question itself seems absurd, out of place, or even archaic. But this contemporary version of faith that works nicely with our vision of success is a bit of a reaction to the Christianity of decades past.

You see, through Christianity's history in America, the church has developed a bad reputation. When unchurched, non-Christian Americans think about Christianity, they may recall the title of Jonathan Edwards' famous sermon, "Sinners in the Hands of an Angry God." They may not know anything about Edwards or the sermon, but they will remember that phrase somehow. Then their minds will flash to overweight preachers bending their bellies over large wooden podiums, screaming something about hell and sin and the evils of rock music. Some might even recall a book called *Turmoil in the Toy Box* that ruined their childhood by convincing their parents that Smurfs were somehow a representation of Satan himself and that to watch the show was tantamount to playing with a Ouija board. At some point, they will think of all the things someone said that God said they couldn't do: wear makeup, play cards, watch movies, drink beer, kiss your date, dance, or crack a smile. (They will be inaccurate, but this is their recollection, so play along.) Picketers outside abortion clinics will come to mind, and with them images of their angry fathers who beat them too harshly, mothers who scolded too constantly, and sermons that made no sense whatsoever. They will be glad for the day they left home, explored the "real world," and became free of what they now call a senseless, self-imposed guilt.

In *Pontoon*, Garrison Keillor paints the perfect portrait of an old woman who grew tired of a stifling, joy-killing, life-sucking religion and decided to live free of her roots. Evelyn grew up in the fictitious town of Lake Wobegon, Minnesota, where Lutherans and Catholics dominate the landscape and shape the culture. But even though Evelyn was part of the church knitting group and known for faithful involvement in church activities, she had a secret life, a life that didn't come to light until after her death. Late in life, after losing her husband to a porn and alcohol addiction, Evelyn reconnects with an old flame. Together they travel the world, staying in fancy hotels and dancing themselves happy.

At first, Barbara, Evelyn's daughter, is horrified by the discovery of her mother's extravagant gallivanting. But as the story unfolds, she stares her own misery in the face and gives up on the Wobegonian practice of ignoring sorrow, stuffing it inside while keeping a steady smile. *My mother is free and is the better for it*, Barbara thought. *She left the shackles of expectations and broke with convention, and she ought to be admired for that.* At Evelyn's ridiculously unorthodox and irreligious "memorial service," Barbara contemplates spelling all this out for everyone, complete with her view of Christians.

> *For a second or two, Barbara considered making a speech of her own—Mother was a free-thinker, it's as simple as that. There is*

no God, we are free agents, each one of us, and if you want to go around with a knapsack of rocks on your back like a person in a cartoon, okay, but I choose to be free, just as my mother, in a lucid moment, wanted you to know that she is free.[3]

To Barbara—as with millions of others—Christians are those who go around with "knapsacks of rocks" on their backs. From a Christian's perspective, it's an unfortunate perception, though we have done things to deserve it. But we know that it is not an accurate representation of Christ and His gospel. The Law, even in the Old Testament, was not the terms for earning a relationship with God; it was the proof of Israel's relationship with God. Think about how the Law was given after God had already rescued Israel from the hand of the Egyptians. So with us, God's commands are not our way into relationship with God but rather the demonstration that a relationship does in fact exist—a relationship that began by His sovereign, gracious act of saving us "while we were still sinners" (Rom. 5:8). We know that every one of us depends on grace—what a wonderful word!—not just for our initial salvation, but for ongoing salvation, the transforming work of the Holy Spirit in us. So understandably, we are troubled by the negative perception others have of Christianity as a life-sucking, joy-killing religion that mandates obedience to an arbitrary set of rules.

It is a valid concern. But I fear we have swung too far. Now we want everyone to know that not only is God not angry with you, He wants to be your personal agent! He wants you to be the best you possible! He wants you to be rich, healthy, living in harmony with everyone, unstressed, not perplexed, well dressed, and always successful! No wonder pro football players are flocking to our mega-churches. *You mean God wants me to make the Pro Bowl every year, even if I have to juice to do it? And God wants to help me get a bigger contract next season—the Almighty is better than Drew Rosenhaus!— even if it encourages greed and selfishness in my heart?* (Of course, they would not likely be that self-aware. And besides, greed and selfishness are not the vices we talk about in church. We prefer the evils of insecurity or not believing in yourself enough.)

I don't know if it's an attempt to genuinely reach pro athletes and wealthy businesspeople or simply a solid plan for growing the church budget, but whatever the case, we've started telling people half-truths. We truthfully proclaim that God wants to bless them and fill their lives with immeasurable joy, but we let them assume— or worse, flat out tell them—that what that means is a bigger house, a better car, a promotion, more sales, and a more robust 401(k). It's a half-truth because, for half the people, that may just be what God wants to do in their lives, and it may come at no cost to their character or commitment to Christ. But for others, it becomes the justification to ignore their families just a little more so they can stay at the office just a little longer so they can get that deal that will give them just enough money to buy that time-share in Kauai.

Poverty and mediocrity are not Christian virtues, nor are they requisites for spiritual growth. But if we're not careful, we can sub-consciously believe that greed is Okay, that selfish ambition is not ungodly, and that as long as I am becoming successful, God must be in it. Yet somewhere along the way, we have added God to a house of idols. Our devotion to Christ is truthfully only one allegiance on a long list of loyalties. We want to rise to influence and be admired by many; we want to live in comfort, with only the "best things for our kids"; we want to be loved by all, validated as a real man or a real woman; we want to retire at fifty-five with several million a year to live on; we want to be remembered as a true pioneer, a trailblazer, a history maker. Oh. And we want to obey and follow Christ. *But I'm sure He wants all those things for us anyway. As a matter of fact, He will bring about all those things—after all, doesn't the Word say that He will give us the desires of our heart?*

Crowded House

This is the second rumor about God: God can be added to my list of loyalties.

I don't need to give up on old goals or loyalties. I just need to add God to them. Joe Smith could have been a money-hungry kid who grew up stealing stuff just to survive on the wrong side of the tracks before He found God and got a sweet job with a fat salary. He still loves money and wants more of it; the only thing different is that now God is going to help him get it. No switch of loyalties. No death to an old way of thinking or living or desiring. Self and self's goals are largely intact. It's just that now God is somehow squeezed into that crowded house.

But enough fictitious examples of this. If I'm looking to find examples of adding God to other goals and allegiances, I need to look no further than my own heart. I would never have said that I consciously added God to other allegiances or idols in my heart, but my heart would betray me.

Why do I feel a sense of pride at how large our church is, and why do I want to keep referencing it when I introduce myself? Why did I feel proud when I saw my pastor at the peak of his influence being interviewed on prime-time national TV? Why did I rejoice in the expanding influence of our church, when what I really was glad for was fame? Why do I keep trying to find a way to work into the conversation how popular my songs are? Why even now am I tempted to tell you which ones I've penned and where they rank on the list of most-sung worship songs? Why is it so hard not to tell everybody all the wonderful things "God is doing in my life"? Why do I imagine that God's will for my life automatically includes record-shattering sales, some kind of award, and global admiration? Why do I feel good about the size of my house?

We have nice words that cloak our pursuits, making us believe they are godly. Influence. Platform. The opportunity to reach more people. These seem noble and Christian, sanctioned—nay, commissioned—by God. But beneath the veneer are the same ugly demons that drive us all: a thirst for success and fame.

The issue is not the circumstance; it's the condition of our heart. Two pastors, arguably, can both have large churches. One is humble, in awe of the supernatural hand of God, careful with how much power he lets accumulate for himself, designing systems and structures that put more people in charge and places others over him and around him. The other's eyes widen every time he takes the stage; he is high-handed and short with others; he dismisses disagreements and runs people through hoops and hierarchies, all of which end with him; every time a crowd applauds or someone gives him an accolade, he gets drunk with his own power. The evil doesn't come from the size of a church, business, or bank account—though growing anything too large where the power resides with just one man is a recipe for self-destruction. The evil comes from our hearts.

> *"Are you still so dull?" Jesus asked them. "Don't you see that whatever enters the mouth goes into the stomach and then out of the body? But the things that come out of the mouth come from the heart, and these make a man 'unclean.' For out of the heart come evil thoughts, murder, adultery, sexual immorality, theft, false testimony, slander." (Matt. 15:16–19)*

When we think of this Scripture, we think of a heart that needs to be reborn. And that is truly the beginning. But it doesn't end with being given a new heart. James, writing to believers, bluntly echoes the reality of an ongoing heart-check:

> *What is causing the quarrels and fights among you? Don't they come from the evil desires at war within you? You want what you don't have, so you scheme and kill to get it. You are jealous of what others have, but you can't get it, so you fight and wage war to take it away from them. Yet you don't have what you want because you don't ask God for it. And even when you ask, you don't get it because your motives are all wrong—you want only what will give you pleasure. (James 4:1–3 NLT)*

Even believers wrestle with an evil, greedy, jealous, angry heart, a heart that only wants what gives pleasure. What makes this mixture even more toxic is that rather than slaying these dragons, we simply add God to the mix. It's not long after that we try to use Him to our same old selfish ends. The desire for fame and success isn't gone; it's just christened as the goal of "reaching more people for Christ." I know rock bands who want to be big, businessmen and businesswomen who want to be rich, and pastors who want to have large churches—all in the name of expanding the kingdom. But deep in their hearts lurks that dark creature, thirsty for fame, hungry for wealth, starving for success. And he is not easily satisfied.

Fractured Hearts

Solomon, long before Jesus and James, warned that we must "keep [our] heart with all diligence, For out of it spring the issues of life" (Prov. 4:23 NKJV). How we live, how we love, how we make our choices—all these and more come from the heart. Yet the most vulnerable spot in all of human life is our hearts. And what our hearts are most prone to is division. It easily follows multiple goals, giving itself to many allegiances. That's why David prayed in Psalm 86, "Teach me your way, O LORD, and I will walk in your truth; give me an *undivided heart*, that I may fear your name" (Ps. 86:11).

Jesus, knowing how quickly and deceptively we follow our impulse for more money, fame, or success, warned, "No servant can serve two masters. Either he will hate the one and love the other, or he will be devoted to the one and despise the other. You cannot serve both God and Money" (Luke 16:13). It's not purely a money issue. Jesus also said that "where your treasure is, there your heart will be also" (Matt. 6:21).

Money is the currency of a world gone mad chasing success and fame. We can't serve God and money because both can't have our hearts. Jesus knows the way we are knit together; He knows the order of life. Luke records these piercing words of Christ:

> *Jesus knew their thoughts and said to them: "Any kingdom divided against itself will be ruined, and a house divided against itself will fall." (Luke 11:17)*

A house divided against itself will fall. A house of idols, home to multiple gods, will be a temple of broken pieces. After the priests of Dagon set the idol upright, back in his place, a more horrific scene met them the next morning.

> *But the next morning the same thing happened—Dagon had fallen face down before the Ark of the Lord again. This time his head and hands had broken off and were lying in the doorway. Only the trunk of his body was left intact. That is why to this day neither the priests of Dagon nor anyone who enters the temple of Dagon in Ashdod will step on its threshold. (1 Sam. 5:4–5 NLT)*

There lay Dagon, the great god of increase and victory, the lord of all gods, the one who gave success, irreparably fractured, humiliatingly broken. There was no way to recover from this. No hiding it. No pretending it didn't happen. From that point on, every time a person stepped into the temple of Dagon, they were reminded of how the mighty Dagon had fallen apart before the great God of Israel.

Our hearts, once divided, cannot stand. Like the idol of Dagon, our lives will break and fracture with our attempt to add God to a list of loyalties. When our hearts become a crowded house of idols—a spiritual temple of Dagon—into which we have tried to squeeze God, our hearts will eventually become like Dagon himself: splintered, shattered, broken.

God doesn't want to be first on a long list of loyalties. He wants to be central, the organizing, unifying core that determines what goes and what stays.

God will not be added to a list of loyalties.

DISCUSSION QUESTIONS:

1. Have you tried to add God to a crowded house of idols? Are you trying to serve God and success?

2. Do you think your heart is divided in its pursuits and desires?

3. What old goals or loyalties in your life need to die?

6. Subversive

Question #2: How Can We Get Rid of This God?

I grew up on a crowded row of houses. They were called "terrace houses," which basically meant each house butted right up against the next one. The houses were made of brick and concrete, so it might be misleading to call it an adjoining wall, but it technically was. The wall proceeded about ten feet out from the entrance before turning into a chain-link fence that kept our front yards or driveways separated. A tall, sturdy gate, complete with a long bolt and a padlock, bounded the driveway. An aluminum awning covered the tiled or terrazzo porch that sat between the walls, shielding it from the rays of the unbearable equatorial sun.

There were no houses across the street from us, just a thirty-foot-wide hilly strip of grass and trees that shielded our neighborhood from a busy road. Our neighbors on one side of our house were sweet, caring

Catholics—a widow with three adult children who lived at home and were quite fond of my sister and me. On the other side was a family with young kids, though I don't remember too much about them. Further down on our street was a Buddhist family with rambunctious boys about my age.

My dad and I used to play badminton over our fence. He would usually let me take the driveway side of the fence because it was sloped to give me the high ground and the much-needed advantage. On one occasion, we took on the rambunctious Buddhist boys in a friendly neighborhood badminton duel. (I must add that if you've never watched competitive, international badminton, you have no idea the ferocity of this sport.)

At the end of our street was a gas station, BP—British Petroleum. I used to walk up there with my sister or my mom and dad to grab a bottle of soda or a bag of chips or simply to replenish my personal supply of instant noodles. Because we were at the far opposite end of the street from the BP station, we would have to walk past almost all the other houses. I remember trying to guess details about the people who lived on our street as we walked by their homes. If a home had a small reddish wooden structure fixed to the wall by the door, a porcelain bowl filled with incense sticks sitting on the structure's shelf, we knew the residents were Buddhists. If an Indian man with an ashy dot on his forehead was pulling into a driveway, we knew he was a Hindu. Inside his home—like the inside of my aunt and uncle's—was sure to be a room veiled by strands of beads with a statue or picture of Krishna fixed on a small altar. If a woman was watering her flowers in her garden, wearing a covering over her head, we knew that family was Muslim. If a home or a family had no distinct markers or altars, we guessed Christian. Sometimes the Christians would make it obvious too, placing a cross on their door or a nice plaque that said, "As for me and my house we will serve the Lord." (That was my family.)

In Malaysia, a person's religion was not a private matter, nor was it a mystery. Belief in God was not something unusual. In fact, I didn't know any atheists growing up except for the mustachioed, slightly overweight American with a jovial laugh who was my dad's boss at the ad agency where he worked. For the most part, the people I was around as a boy believed in God or in a god or a host of gods. Nonreligion was virtually nonexistent.

American Idols

All the major religions of the world are at home in Malaysia—not that any of them began there, but all of them are widely practiced. Needless to say, idols abound. In a culture where people actually have to renounce the idol-worshipping religion of their parents and ancestors in order to become a Christian, churches speak of idolatry as something literally connected to the relics and practices of Buddhism or Hinduism.

For most Americans, though, that sort of idolatry is a foreign concept. The vast majority of us don't have bronze statues of a fat bald man sitting cross-legged on our mantles. In fact, unless you've been on a mission trip or live in the great state of California, you've probably never seen a statue of Buddha in real life. But idols are common to every culture. The gods of ambition, success, victory, strength, and dominance are the things we serve as though they were immortal and had the power to bestow that immortality to us.

Ernest Becker in *Escape from Evil* cuts to the heart of it, calling out the "immortality symbols" we pursue:

> *Money gives power now—and, through accumulated property, land, and interest, power in the future.... The symbols of immortal power that money buys exist on the level of the visible, and so crowd out their invisible competitor.... No wonder economic equality is beyond the imagination of modern, democratic man: the house, the car, the bank balance are his immortality symbols.*[1]

David Goetz, a former editor for *Christianity Today*, takes it a step further, warning that even pastors are not exempt:

> *For clergy, it's the three-thousand-member mega-church. I wrote and edited for a clergy publication for several years. I often sat in the studies of both small-church pastors and mega-church pastors, listening to their stories, their hopes, their plans for significance.... Religious professionals went into ministry for the significance, to make an impact, called by God to make a difference with their lives. But when you're fifty-three and serving a congregation of 250, you know, finally, you'll never achieve the large-church immortality symbol.*[2]

Goetz goes on about how our culture prizes the possession of immortality symbols:

> *There is, frankly, no one more uninteresting than a person with no immortality symbols: the suburban family with no smart or*

athletic kids that lives in a relatively small house; the poor; the
single mom left to raise three kids under twelve after the divorce;
the elderly with no winter condo in Florida; the head of house-
hold with no real career track; the midlife pastor with a small
congregation. None of these folks is asked to speak at the college
alumni banquet.[3]

Our quest for immortality symbols is a clue that even in our age of science and modernity, we are guilty of idol worship. We hide invisible idols in our hearts. I'm not sure who has a harder time believing in these invisible idols—a culture with literal stone idols or a culture with none. In a culture with literal idols like Malaysia, a new Christian can become so satisfied with her renunciation of sacred shrines and stone idols that she forgets to look in her heart for the love of money. But then again, in a culture like America where literal idols are rarely seen, we tend not to pay any attention to idolatry as a vice at all.

Here are a few things we learn about idols and idolatry from Scripture:

- Idols are the work of a man's hands (Ps. 115:4; Ps. 135:15; Is. 2:8; Hab. 2:18)
- Idols are made out of natural, earthly materials such as wood, silver, and gold (Deut. 29:17)
- Idols are worthless (Is. 44:9; Jer. 2:5, 8; Jer. 8:19)
- Idols can't speak, must be carried, and can do no harm or good (Jer. 10:5)
- Idols are a fraud (Jer. 51:17)

- Idolatry is exchanging the glory of the one true God for something that is utterly worthless and false (Jer. 2:11)
- Idolatry defiles a person (Ez. 20:7,18, 31; Ez. 22:3, 4; Ez. 23:7)

From these key statements in Scripture about idolatry, we can conclude that an idol is something we've made with human ingenuity out of the stuff of life and treated as God, though it is false, worthless, and powerless. This could be taking something that isn't God and treating it like a god, like the love of or allegiance to money or success. This is the form of idolatry we are more familiar with. Youth pastors warn their students about the perils of making a sport or a band they love or dating itself into an idol. An idol, the sermon goes, is anything we place above God, anything we love, value, or devote our time and attention to more than Jesus. Certainly, there is truth to this, as Paul affirms in Colossians 3:5: "Put to death, therefore, whatever belongs to your earthly nature: sexual immorality, impurity, lust, evil desires and greed, which is idolatry." Or as one translation words the latter half: "Don't be greedy, for a greedy person is an idolater, worshiping the things of this world" (NLT).

But idolatry has another, subtler, far more insidious side. Idolatry can also be taking God and describing Him, forming Him, making Him into an image that He is not. This is the lesser-known variation, yet probably the more common reality in America. We want a god that is like us, a god that loves like we do, that values what we value—a god fashioned after our own image. This is the god of ambiguous spirituality, the great Spirit of the Universe, the god who is only love and never judgment, the god of Oprah, Eckhart Tolle, and Universalism. This is the god of subjective reality, who lets each person define him as they please, according to their experience or convenience. He is the god of false peace, who promises harmony in the world if we admit that we are all after the same thing and that all roads must in the end lead there.

Holy Cow(s)

There was a king of Israel named Jeroboam who committed precisely this kind of idolatry, and it was forever held against him. In fact, it was such a severe idolatry that the writer of 1 and 2 Kings repeatedly references Jeroboam and his sin and the sin he "had caused Israel to commit" (1 Kings 15:26 is the first time the phrase is used, but it occurs throughout both 1 and 2 Kings). He was credited as the one who "enticed Israel away from following the LORD and caused them to commit a great sin" (2 Kings 17:21). No doubt, Israel had a part to play. They "persisted in all the sins of Jeroboam and did not turn away from them" (2 Kings 17:22). But Jeroboam started it. And to God, that matters immensely. Wicked kings after Jeroboam are measured against Jeroboam's wickedness (around fifteen references), and even good kings—or the not so wicked ones—are evaluated on how much of Jeroboam's sin they reversed.[4]

So what was it? What was the evil that Jeroboam did?

A little context first. When Solomon died, his son Rehoboam inherited the throne. The people had been taxed, burdened, and overworked under Solomon because of all his building projects. They asked Rehoboam if he would consider lightening the load. Rehoboam consulted with the older, wiser counselors who had been with his father. They recommended giving the people a break. Then Rehoboam decided to ask his young, peer advisors. They said, in essence, "Forget mercy. Tell the people if they thought it was bad back then, it's going to be far worse now. Assert your power and strength, show them that you're a tougher ruler." Rehoboam took their counsel. The ten tribes from the north revolted, turning to former military leader and fan favorite Jeroboam, who had recently returned from exile. The ten tribes in the north crowned Jeroboam king and retained the name "Israel" over their territories. Rehoboam held onto the two southern tribes of Judah and Benjamin; they called themselves the nation of Judah. From that moment in history, the kingdom of Israel, once victorious under David and glorious under Solomon, was divided.

Jeroboam's first problem was dealing with potential defectors. Jerusalem, the site of the temple and the only location for the worship of Yahweh, was in the southern kingdom of Judah. If his people kept traveling down there for important festivals and special worship occasions, they might eventually want to stay. Besides, Rehoboam and Jeroboam didn't like each other and would rather not have their people cross paths.

Jeroboam's solution was to set up alternate worship sites, and while he was at it, why not make two sites in Israel instead of one? So in Bethel and in Dan, Jeroboam built altars of worship. As if that weren't bad enough, he crafted two golden calves to be at each site to symbolize the God they served.

Jeroboam thought to himself, "Unless I am careful, the kingdom will return to the dynasty of David. When these people

go to Jerusalem to offer sacrifices at the Temple of the LORD,
they will again give their allegiance to King Rehoboam of
Judah. They will kill me and make him their king instead."
So on the advice of his counselors, the king made two gold
calves. He said to the people, "It is too much trouble for
you to worship in Jerusalem. Look, Israel, these are the gods
who brought you out of Egypt!" He placed these calf idols in
Bethel and in Dan—at either end of his kingdom. But this
became a great sin, for the people worshiped the idols, travel-
ing as far north as Dan to worship the one there. (1 Kings
12:26–30 NLT)

To be fair, Jeroboam was probably imitating the example of
Aaron so many years before at Sinai when Moses took forever to
come down from meeting with God. Remember? Aaron took gold
from the people's jewelry, crafted a golden calf, and said, "O Israel,
these are the gods who brought you out of the land of Egypt!"
(Ex. 32:4 NLT).

Jeroboam's sin was taking the one true, glorious God—
Yahweh—and shaping Him into an image that He is not. He
fashioned God into something he imagined and created—not to
mention something he created out of a desire for political security
and personal gain. Jeroboam's version of God did not meet God's
own descriptions of Himself, and the worship Jeroboam set up for
this "God" did not meet the worship requirements God Himself
had prescribed. Jeroboam's idolatry didn't have to do with loving
something more than God as much as it had to do with a faulty
God-concept.

Trojan Horse

If idolatry is defined as treating something that isn't God as if it were or forming God into in an image that He is not, then we would find ourselves guilty on both counts.

We have kept a host of loyalties in our lives, treating desires and drives of this world as though they are worthy of worship. What's more, by believing that God can keep company with such competing allegiances in our hearts, we have created a Christianity that finds itself in the company of strangers. Eckhart Tolle, pop religion's great teacher of the harmony of all religions, insists that his hodgepodge philosophy of New Age stew is completely compatible with Christianity.[5] I recommend not getting upset with Eckhart, but rather with the churches that led him to believe that. What in the world are we preaching that makes a New Age universalist think that his way is compatible with Christianity? We've worked so hard at making Christianity palatable to the world that the world has stolen our sermon notes. And they're preaching it better than we are.

I am stunned at how many overlapping phrases the teachers of *The Secret* have with Christian prosperity preachers. Rhonda Byrnes, the author of the best-selling book *The Secret,* teaches that "without exception every human being has the ability to transform any weakness or suffering into strength, power, perfect peace, health and abundance."[6] Sound familiar? Yes, the best falsehoods contain morsels of truth, but the best lies also repeat other lies. *You can create your own reality. You can have immeasurable wealth. You can always be the top and never the bottom, a success that never feels the agony of defeat.* The "secret" is in the confession or the belief firmly entrenched in your heart and mind, a sort of "seed you sow" into the universe that now turns the energy of the world in your favor. *The Secret* seems like nothing more than the best prosperity gospel messages without mentioning Jesus or taking an offering.

Perhaps we have paid so much attention to making Christianity relevant to culture that we've forgotten how it is designed to flow in opposition to it. We have allowed our quest for immortality symbols to coexist with our Christianity, resulting in a faith that is foreign to the one Christ came to initiate. Christ came speaking the language of His culture, fully intent on undermining it. We come speaking the language of our culture with the secret hope of being loved by it.

Remember the words of Christ:

If the world hates you, remember that it hated me first. The world would love you as one of its own if you belonged to it, but you are no longer part of the world. I chose you to come out of the world, so it hates you. (John 15:18–19 NLT)

Moments earlier, Jesus had announced, "I am the way and the truth and the life. No one comes to the Father except through me" (John 14:6).

On a different occasion, He adjusted their expectations by saying, "Don't imagine that I came to bring peace to the earth! I came not to bring peace, but a sword" (Matt. 10:34 NLT).

These are the forgotten words of Christ. These are the words that don't allow you to paint Christ as a peace-loving Galilean country bumpkin who embraces everyone like a hippie at Woodstock. These are the words that reveal a Christ whom Paul later described as a stumbling block for the Jews and foolishness to the Gentiles (1 Cor. 1:23). These are the glimpses in the Gospels that foreshadow the Jesus of Revelation, the One whose face shines like the sun, the One with a sword coming out of His mouth.

To imagine a Zenlike Jesus at peace with Himself, unwilling to harm a fly, is to miss the incredibly subversive mission of Christ on earth. He came as a baby in a dingy stable to become ruler over all; He came as an overlooked carpenter who would renovate our hearts; He came to undermine the religious establishment while fulfilling the Law they claimed to follow; He came to die as a filthy criminal so He could be the Savior of the world. He came to shouts in the streets and victory chants and cries of "Hosanna!" while making claims like "Take up your cross! Deny yourself! Sell all you have and give it to the poor! Eat my flesh and drink my blood!"

He came like a Trojan horse, welcomed as a gift yet bound to lead us to our death. But this subversion is the means to His ends, for in our death we find His life.

No Other Gods

As the subversive Jesus begins to drill into our hearts, striking at the root of our pride, selfishness, and greed, a choice becomes clear: Will it be Jesus and His will, or me and mine?

For the Philistines, they had to choose: Will it be Yahweh or Dagon? The surprising conclusion to the story—and maybe it is telling of the propensity of our own hearts—is that despite all the Philistines had seen, they chose to keep Dagon. They chose to keep the god who had fallen, broken, in front of Israel's God. Twice. For a culture that was likely superstitious and unlikely to believe in coincidence, choosing Dagon after all that had happened was like buying more stock in Enron after the scandal broke. It was an utter denial of reality.

But they had no choice. It seemed that God—the true God—was against them, bent on their destruction.

Then the LORD's heavy hand struck the people of Ashdod and the nearby villages with a plague of tumors. When the people realized what was happening, they cried out, "We can't keep the Ark of the God of Israel here any longer! He is against us! We will all be destroyed along with Dagon, our god." (1 Sam. 5:6–7 NLT)

For a New Testament believer, we know that because of Christ, God is no longer against us. If we are in Christ, we are a new creation, we are justified—declared righteous—we are holy and accepted by God. Grace comes to us as salvation from the penalty of sin through the life, death, and resurrection of Jesus Christ, but it also comes as salvation from the power of sin through the work of the Holy Spirit in our lives. There is a sense in which God is bent on our "destruction." He wants to destroy our flesh, our sinful desires, which John describes as "the lust of the flesh, the lust of the eyes, and the pride of life" (1 John 2:16 NKJV). He is on a mission of destruction that will end up being our salvation. God means to work like an antidote against the toxin of sin in our heart. He intends to operate on us like a cancer surgeon, methodically and doggedly determined to excavate every cell that would cause our

eternal demise. So, in that sense, the question the Philistines asked
is still one we must answer:

*"What should we do with the Ark of the God of Israel?" (1 Sam.
5:8 NLT)*

What do we do with this God? What should we do with the God
who wants total and absolute control of our hearts? If we're honest, our
question might more closely resemble *The Message* translation: "How
can we get rid of the chest of the god of Israel?" (1 Sam. 5:8 MSG).

We have the choice: Get rid of God or get rid of Dagon and
friends. We can, like the Philistines, choose a god we know to be false
simply because it is safe and we don't want to be destroyed. Or we
can welcome the holy destruction of sin and every root of it in our
hearts as we allow God to do His work.

We must let Him have His way, totally and completely. Let Him
expose our pride, our selfishness. Let Him unearth our motives. Let
Him show us when we are doing things—even or especially good,
noble, godly things like caring for the sick or feeding the poor and
homeless—because we want to be noticed or praised or admired.
Remember that the same Jesus who healed and told the cured to keep
it a secret, the same Jesus who at the peak of His popularity gave His
most offensive and enigmatic sermon, the same Jesus who urged us to
give in secret—this Jesus is at work in our hearts. He won't let us get
away with simply the right behavior; He wants innocent hearts, full of
love and humility. There can be no other gods of fame and influence
that we keep paying homage to, hoping to gain immortality.

But there is more.

We are tempted to get rid of "this God," the God who makes idols crumble, the God of not only mercy and love but also of justice, truth, and judgment. We don't say aloud that we want to get rid of God, but we keep searching for ways to make God more palatable. It is evident in the increasingly popular attempts to envision a "kinder Christianity." Insomuch as those attempts offer a correction to an American right-wing Christian culture that has gone awry in legalism and self-righteousness, I applaud the effort. But if these new visions of Christianity mean—and I'm not sure if they do—to take the edge out of Christ's words—literally, take the sword out of His mouth—or remove the unmistakably subversive intentions that Jesus has of ruling our hearts exclusively, then it may be something you would deem worthy of belief, but it would not be Christianity.

To truly embrace "this God" means that we must be rid not only of the things we worship as idols but also of the idol we have made and called "God." It is not enough to lay aside greed, pride, and the like; we must resist the kind of idolatry that fashions God simply into an image we desire or relate to instead of the God He reveals Himself through Jesus and Scripture to be.

This is what it means to have no other gods before the one and only God.

You

I have begun to ask myself a question that I would have never dared to ask before: What if Jesus has a different goal for my life than I do?

I'm not talking about the kind of goals that have to do with career moves or a life's work. I'm talking about goals as in a general direction, as in the goal of progress, improvement, the thing we call success, the goals of getting more, doing more, being more, the goals of moving upward, forward, and onward. I have been accustomed to a Jesus who cooperates with me and those goals, the Jesus who wants me to have more open doors, more stuff, and more happy experiences.

As I have asked myself that question over and over for the past few years, I have begun to see Jesus again. Not a Jesus who wants to make me miserable or poor because that is somehow more noble or pure. But also not a Jesus who automatically works for my general advancement and improvement in this world. Not a Jesus of sadistic intentions, but also not a Jesus of suburban values.

I've begun to see the Jesus of the Gospels, who came to turn the understood notion of religion and how it works on its head—the Jesus who forced people to reconsider their rationale for their routines; the Jesus who challenged values and socially accepted vices and virtues. This is a subversive Jesus. This is a King whose humble birth and friendly demeanor concealed His true agenda of ruling our lives. This faith that we have embraced, this Life that we have taken into our hearts, will be our undoing. It is designed to be the end of us. The Jesus I've come to see and know at work in my life is the One who comes to undermine my own small-minded and wrongheaded plans. He is the Trojan horse of blessing that we readily welcome into our hearts without knowing His mission to destroy our old way of life. And He won't stop until He has every part of our hearts. I've said that before, but I am starting to realize what that might really mean. It means He will do everything in His power—everything—to make us His. So if giving us stuff achieves that goal, then so be it. But if allowing things to be taken away gets us there quicker, He just may opt for that route. He is our friend in the way that we have never fully understood a friend to be—one who will act for our good even when we don't see it as good.

As with everything that God requires of us, allowing God to dethrone our many allegiances and fully and firmly establish His exclusive rule in our hearts works for His glory and for our good. When we persist in idolatry by calling something God that He is not, we are not only robbing Him of the glory He is worthy of, but we are also robbing ourselves of the good He designed us for. The real danger of sending the subversive Jesus away is that we miss the power of His grace.

Jonah so beautifully prayed, "Those who cling to worthless idols forfeit the grace that could be theirs" (Jonah 2:8).

There is a grace that saved you and will keep saving you if you allow it to, if you yield to it and let it have its way. For all the blessings, opportunities, healings, miracles, provisions, protections, and stability that God has given you, there is one thing that He values more, one thing that He would trade all of the above for: you.

He is after you.

So if you haven't yet experienced the doors of the great wooden horse bursting open with warriors bent on your defeat, wait. It's coming. And when it does, when Christ comes to save your life by leading you to lose it, embrace Him. Embrace Him again as you did at first when you thought Christianity was all about your happiness. Embrace His work. Count it all joy.

It will save your life.

Again.

DISCUSSION QUESTIONS:

1. Have you ever treated something that isn't God as if it were?

2. How have you made God in your image?

3. Is it possible that God has different goals for your life than you do? How so?

7. Audacity

Rumor #3: God Is Pleased with My Goodness.

"Be a good boy, Glenn," my aunt used to say to me. "Finish your dinner. Listen to Mommy and Daddy. Be a good boy, Glenn."

My aunt was a Hindu.

Like so many others in Malaysia who were deeply religious, my aunt believed that the point of all religion was to make you good. So it didn't matter that we were Christians and she was a Hindu; to her, we all had the same goal: to become better people. This, of course, was not necessarily sound theology, even for her. In fact, many others on my dad's side of the family took years before they would extend anything beyond common human courtesy to him—and us.

But Aunty Thana was different. She was kind and always warm. She refused to allow a difference in religion to become a barrier between family and her. She believed there was some common thread that could allow us to get along. Actually, that belief is what allows for the harmony among various races and religions in Malaysia and in many other cultures of diversity. So long as it does not involve family members changing religions—that would be dishonoring to the family name—let people believe whatever they want to believe.

With one important caveat: that the belief is not destructive; that it is not harmful; that it makes society better; that it makes us *good* people.

Regardless of what you believe, you are free to believe it if it makes you a better person. Goodness seems to be the common goal of any legitimate religion.

Goodness in America looks a little like Jack.

Jack has been a schoolteacher for about twenty years. History, technically, is what he teaches, but he was hired because of his coaching prowess. So, he's a history/gym teacher/basketball coach. But Jack often goes the extra mile. He's been known to single out so-called "problem students" and meet with them after school hours, serving as a life coach and mentor. He has even taken the trouble to get to know their parents, who insist they have no clue why their little angel is acting up. Jack doesn't just do his job. Jack cares about his job and works tirelessly at it.

Jack and his family go to church. There are several Bibles in Jack's house, though few if any are ever read. It is more a symbol of a good home than a book to be devoured. Jack rarely speaks of God, except when he invokes a blessing on America. Still, Jack is a *good* man. Where Jack lives, no one really talks about being "born again" or "making Jesus Lord and Savior." Everybody believes in God, goes to church, and roots for the Cowboys. If Jack died today, the whole county would come out to his funeral. They would talk about Jack's service to the community, about his love for his family, and about that brown trout he caught one summer at the lake.

Nobody would question even for a second if Jack was in heaven. *Of course he is. Peter is probably showing him the best places for fishing right now!* If open mic eulogies were allowed, people would take turns telling their favorite stories about Jack, and no doubt, this phrase would keep falling off their lips: *He was a good man.*

You probably know Jack. Strong. Reliable. Tough. Consistent. Steady.

Good.

Christianity in America tends to resemble the spirit of the pioneers, those hardy souls who sailed across the Atlantic to the New World, and those brave, determined ones who headed further west and homesteaded through dust bowls and brutal winters. A Christian in America is the epitome of this tireless ethic. A Christian is a person who works hard at improving his behavior, has mastered the art of filtering out bad thoughts, and keeps showing up at church every Sunday. The pastor might give a nice talk on how Jesus taught us to love one another and so maybe this week we should bake a pie for our neighbors or give an elderly woman your seat on the bus. The gospel is that God is good, so we ought to be too. And if we fail, well, try not to do it again, and let's just not talk about it. Sin, sorrow, temptation, and doubt are easily hidden behind a firm handshake and a stiff smile.

We are, after all, *good* people.

Good People

Regardless of our culture, story, or religion, there seems to be something in all of us that makes us want to be better people. If goodness is the common goal of religion, then progress is the common pursuit of humanity. Every new year is a new chance to renew our vows to lose weight, spend more time with our families, go to church more regularly, give more money to good causes, and watch less TV. That is not a bad impulse. It probably is some evidence of the *imago Dei* in us. We are made in God's image and want to do Godlike things. The problem comes not in desiring to do such things but in believing that we are capable of those things.

I was at a small group recently with several couples in their forties and fifties, discussing the topic of evangelism. After going a few rounds talking about how we can each do more to reach the people around us, someone lamented that the biggest obstacle we face is the common perception of Christians as hypocrites.

We have such a bad witness, someone lamented.

I mean, our divorce rate is the same as those in the world.

And our kids behave just as badly.

How can we tell people about Jesus when we don't live like Him?

These are common complaints, and they have crippled Christians for decades. But they belie a more troubling presupposition: Christianity is about behavior modification. Being a Christian means acting better than a non-Christian.

This presupposed definition shows up in our approach in several ways. When we judge "sinners," we point at their poor behavior, their drunken habits or vulgar language or frivolous morality—and we do so from a seat of security, confidence, in our own good behavior. We are like the man Jesus described who prayed, "God, I thank you that I am not like other men" (Luke 18:11). This is why, when our own behavior is poor, we feel we have lost grounds for speaking to others about changing their lives. Good behavior is the source for our authority to speak to "lost people."

But the presupposition that Christianity is about behavior modification also shows up in the way we try to approach God. If we've had a good week, if we've read our Bibles some or haven't had a fight with our spouse or yelled at the kids or kicked the dog, then we come to church with our heads held high. We have been a good Christian this week. We can worship, we can clap, we can sing, we can throw our heads back and laugh a good, hearty laugh. This has been a good week. But when we've struggled, when we've wrestled with doubt or walked through difficulty or lost our tempers, then being at church makes us feel out of place. We don't belong here. We're just not good Christians.

In short, our belief that Christianity is about good behavior affects the way we approach others and it affects the way we approach God.

God Comes Home

We are not the first to put that much stake in our good behavior. Let's return to the story of the ark.

When the Philistines had enough of the boils and tumors that struck their people after the whole falling Dagon episode, they decided it was time to get rid of the ark for good. Seven months of turmoil was more than they could bear. When they asked their own priests and diviners what they should do and how they could send the ark away, the priests instructed them to send a guilt offering of five gold tumors and five gold rats to represent the five rulers of the Philistine lands afflicted by the outbreak of tumors and boils. Then they told the people to plan an exit that would be a sign for them of whether or not it was the God of Israel that had struck them or whether it was simply coincidental. (Even ancient pagans wrestled with doubt.)

> *Now build a new cart, and find two cows that have just given birth to calves. Make sure the cows have never been yoked to a cart. Hitch the cows to the cart, but shut their calves away from them in a pen. Put the Ark of the LORD on the cart, and beside it place a chest containing the gold rats and gold tumors you are sending as a guilt offering. Then let the cows go wherever they want. If they cross the border of our land and go to Beth-shemesh, we will know it was the LORD who brought this great disaster upon us. If they don't, we will know it was not his hand that caused the plague. It came simply by chance. (1 Sam. 6:7–9 NLT)*

The Philistines did as their priest had instructed, placing the ark and the chest of gold rats and tumors all on a cart driven by cows who had never been yoked and had just given birth. "And sure enough, without veering off in other directions, the cows went straight along the road toward Beth-shemesh, lowing as they went" (1 Samuel 6:12a NLT).

When the Israelites in Beth-shemesh saw the ark approaching, their hearts leaped with joy. This was a glorious day! As dark as the day was when the ark had been captured, this was a day of great rejoicing. God had come home. They broke the wood of the cart to kindle a fire, killed the cows, sacrificing them as a burnt offering to the Lord. In their midst were a few Levites—the ones who had been set apart to handle the ark and carry out priestly duties. The Levites at Beth-shemesh carried the ark and set it on a rock, in an elevated place for all to view. Then the people offered more sacrifices and burnt offerings, all while the five Philistine rulers watched. The plan had worked. It was indeed the God of Israel who had struck the Philistines, and now the curse had lifted; the ark of the God of Israel had returned where He belonged.

Looking at the Law

But after the Philistines went home, something strange happened in Beth-shemesh. The people had gotten curious or careless or irreverent. We're unsure of their reason or motive. The Bible simply says this:

> But the LORD killed seventy men from Beth-shemesh because they looked into the Ark of the LORD. And the people mourned greatly because of what the LORD had done. (1 Sam. 6:19 NLT)

They opened up the cover of the ark of the covenant and looked inside. And God struck them dead. *What the heck is going on?* What did they do wrong?

The first step to finding an answer is in discovering what was *in* the ark. What could they have seen that was so sacred?

According to Hebrews 9:4, the ark contained three items: the Law, the pot of manna, and Aaron's rod that had budded. But the only thing the Old Testament specifically records was placed inside the ark were the tablets on which Moses inscribed the Ten Commandments.

Then I came back down the mountain and put the tablets in the ark I had made, as the LORD commanded me, and they are there now. (Deut. 10:5)

Shortly before, the pot of manna was placed "in front of the Testimony" to be a reminder of God's provision (Ex. 16:34). And after the tablets of the Law were placed inside the ark, the Lord instructed Moses to place Aaron's rod that had budded also "in front of the Testimony" to remind people not to grumble against the Lord (Num. 17:10).[1] But the Ten Commandments were the first thing placed in the ark—the only thing the Old Testament clearly states was placed inside it—and later, in Solomon's day, they are again listed as the only item in the ark.[2]

From these passages, it seems that the Law was clearly the main item in the ark. In fact, it's pretty likely that the only thing the men at Beth-shemesh saw when they removed the cover from the ark was the Law.

Hold that thought. Now, let's talk for a moment about the cover of the ark of the covenant. The ark was a large wooden box with gold overlaying the inside and outside, gold molding around it, and four gold rings at each bottom corner for the poles that were used to carry the ark. The cover, or "Atonement cover," as it was called, was much more ornate. It was made of solid gold. On top of it was a figure of two angels—the cherubim—made from hammered gold, molded as one giant piece with the cover itself. The angels faced each other, with heads bowed down toward the atonement cover. "There, above the cover between the two cherubim that are over the ark of the Testimony, I [God] will meet with you and give you all my commands for the Israelites" (Ex. 25:22).

Above the cover, between the angels, is where God would speak to Moses. It was also where Aaron, the high priest, would sprinkle the blood of a bull and a goat when he entered the Holy of Holies one day of the year—Yom Kippur, the Day of Atonement. The atonement cover was called that because that's where the blood was sprinkled to atone for all of Israel's sins on the Day of Atonement (Lev. 16:14–15).

The ark was so sacred that even the high priest could not go into the Holy of Holies whenever he wanted, and even on the specified day—the Day of Atonement—there were no guarantees that he would not be struck down if he failed to follow God's instructions (Lev. 16:13). (That's why the high priestly garments had bells on the edges—they could tell if the movement had stopped.)

Now, here's the punch: *To lift the cover of the ark of the covenant is to stare the law of God in the face without the cover of blood.* It is to say that you are holy enough, good enough, to handle God's law without the mercy of God's forgiveness or the atoning power of the blood.

This is the third rumor we believe about God: *God is pleased with my goodness.*

Good Enough

I don't know anyone who would say it quite that way. If a person doesn't believe in God, then good behavior is just something that benefits society and helps you "win friends and influence people." If a person believes in God, but not necessarily in Jesus as the only way to God, then good behavior is what God expects of us and is simply something we're supposed to have, and if we have more good behavior than bad behavior, we get better karma or eternal rewards, or we get heaven instead of hell. This is why many people I know simply can't buy the "Jesus" thing. *I don't need a Savior. I'm a pretty good guy. Christianity is a crutch for the weak-minded or those with low self-esteem or those who have just lived a terrible life. But me—I'm a good guy.*

The good people have the hardest time swallowing the message of the cross, because they would never classify themselves as sinners. In my city, there are thousands of good people—*Jacks.* People who work hard, try to do the right thing, and vote with conservative, family-friendly values. Many of them probably don't go to church, but instead take their kids to the park, or grill burgers with some friends. Good people. Some of them probably do go to church— some probably to my church. Here is where things can get tricky. After all, maybe what's worse than thinking you don't need to be a Christian is thinking you already are one because you act like one— at times, even better.

The trap becomes more dangerous the closer it gets to truth.

There is a sort of ignorance that comes from severe unfamiliarity with God and His holiness that makes a person think that he is capable of pleasing the holy, infinite God who created everything. But there is also a kind of deception that comes from overfamiliarity with God that leads a person down the same path. The group that just might have the hardest time believing that they cannot please God through behavior is longtime Christians.

Longtime Christians—and I am one of them—are those born into a Christian family. We have no dramatic "testimony." While high school friends were out drinking and partying, we were memorizing Bible verses and playing Scrabble; when others zoned out to Nirvana, we pepped up with dc Talk. We learned the rules early and had perfected the art of following them by the time we completed our last AP class. We don't cuss, we don't chew, we don't hang with girls who do.

I don't for a second regret my Christian roots. I'm grateful for godly parents and am glad to have been spared the heartache so many others had to endure. I'm not ashamed about being a longtime Christian at all; the truth is, I'm proud of it.

But that's just it. If I'm honest, I'm so proud of it, I almost think I deserve this grace. I think that God made a wise investment sending His Son to die for me. *Good move, God. I would have done the same thing.* We sing "Amazing Grace" while echoing the refrain of the L'Oreal commercial in our hearts: *because I'm worth it!* We have inverted the gospel of grace, which says, "I am worthy because Christ died for me," to mean "Christ died for me because I'm worthy." There is a massive difference between the two. We act as if all we needed was another try. And we think that because, deep down, we believe that we are good enough.

Americans are in love with second chances. We love when the

Red Sox—who hadn't been able to beat the Yankees in a playoff series in decades—got one more crack at it and came back from a three to one deficit to reach and eventually win the World Series. The only thing better than a rags-to-riches story is a riches-to-rags-to-riches story. We love how Thomas Edison tried ninety-nine wrong ways before finally inventing the lightbulb. What all the people in these great success stories needed was one more try, one more shot, one more opportunity for greatness.

America was settled by many who thought that way. Society in Europe was oppressive. Many were not able to live according to their conscience or break out of economic servitude. So they came to the New World for one more chance. Here they could buy land, raise livestock, and chart their own destiny. America became home not just of the brave, but of the self-made.

In a way, that's how many Christians view their salvation. *We were down. We'd made some bad choices. But everyone does, right? Thankfully, God kept believing in us, and gave us a second chance. Hallelujah! He's the God of second chances! And that's all we needed. We're back on our feet now! Praise the Lord!* Grace is a sort of canceling of debts and a fresh influx of capital to try the business venture one more time. It's as if we say, *Thank You for saving me, Lord. I'll take it from here.*

But grace is not just a second chance. If it were, it would not be that amazing, because no matter how hard we try or how many times we try, we cannot fully please God. We simply do not have the ability. The truth—and it is painful to admit—is that no matter how good we are, we will never be good enough to satisfy God's holiness. And that doesn't change even after becoming a Christian.

The Impossible Task

When Jesus walked the earth, there was a group of people who had devoted their lives to obeying the law. They were called "Pharisees." It is uncertain where the name exactly came from, though some have suggested they were called "separatists" (our word "Pharisee" comes from the Greek *pharisaios,* which likely finds its roots in the Aramaic *perushim,* meaning "separate") as a derogatory label from their adversaries.[3] The Pharisees didn't stop with a strict observance of the Torah; they had their own purity laws that they observed. In fact, according to the Talmud, there were seven kinds of Pharisees:

1. The Shechemite Pharisee: One who simply kept the law for what he could profit thereby. (Named after Shechem in the Old Testament who submitted to circumcision to obtain Dinah.)
2. The Humbling Pharisee: One who appeared to be humble by always hanging down his head.
3. The Bleeding Pharisee: One who walked with his eyes closed so as not to see a woman but ended up running into things and bleeding.
4. The Mortar Pharisee: One who wore a mortar-shaped cap to cover his eyes so he wouldn't see any impurities or indecencies.
5. The What-Am-I-To-Do-Yet Pharisee: One who didn't know much about the law, but as soon as he was done completing one task, asked, "What is my duty now?"

6. The Pharisee from Fear: One who kept the law because he was afraid of future judgment.

7. The Pharisee from Love: One who obeyed the Lord because he loved Him with all his heart.[4]

It's easy to vilify the Pharisees. They are the closest things to villains in the Gospels. But before we rush to Jesus' indicting words to them—there are many, and we will get there—it is good to see that these were men who loved God. They are to be admired for their incredible conviction and courage. They stood against the grain, refused to be tainted by political motives like the Zealots, and were unwilling to sell out in the face of incredible opposition.

The Pharisees in Jesus' day were widely respected. They held a place of influence not because of any office or function but simply because people admired them. They were the radicals, the obedient ones, the faithful.

But they had one fatal flaw: They thought they could impress God with their good behavior, their moral reform, their disciplined and rigorous efforts.

Jesus was tough on the Pharisees. In His famous diatribe against them, recorded in Matthew 23, Jesus declared:

Woe to you, teachers of the law and Pharisees, you hypocrites!
You shut the kingdom of heaven in men's faces. You yourselves
do not enter, nor will you let those enter who are trying to.
Woe to you, teachers of the law and Pharisees, you hypocrites!
You travel over land and sea to win a single convert, and
when he becomes one, you make him twice as much a son of
hell as you are. (Matt. 23:13–15)

He continued:

*Woe to you, teachers of the law and Pharisees, you hypo-
crites! You clean the outside of the cup and dish, but inside
they are full of greed and self-indulgence. Blind Pharisee!
First clean the inside of the cup and dish, and then the
outside also will be clean. Woe to you, teachers of the law
and Pharisees, you hypocrites! You are like whitewashed
tombs, which look beautiful on the outside but on the inside
are full of dead men's bones and everything unclean. In the
same way, on the outside you appear to people as righteous
but on the inside you are full of hypocrisy and wickedness.
(Matt. 23:25–28)*

But in a way, Jesus was tough on the rest of us too.

In the Sermon on the Mount, Jesus said, "Unless your righteousness surpasses that of the Pharisees and the teachers of the law, you
will certainly not enter the kingdom of heaven" (Matt. 5:20).

And again, in the same sermon He said, "Be perfect, therefore,
as your heavenly Father is perfect" (Matt. 5:48).

When the rich man asked Jesus what he was still lacking and
Jesus instructed him to sell all he had and give it to the poor, the man
walked away sad, and Jesus said to the crowd, "Children, how hard it
is to enter the kingdom of God! It is easier for a camel to go through
the eye of a needle than for a rich man to enter the kingdom of God"
(Mark 10:24–25).

How is it possible? How can my righteousness exceed the righteousness of the Pharisees? How can a rich man enter the kingdom

of heaven if a camel could never enter the eye of a needle? (By the way, the rumor that there was a gate in Jerusalem called the "Needle's Eye" is pure speculation, surfacing as a theory as late as the eleventh century!)

Jesus appears to be asking the impossible. Indeed, He is. Living the way God wants us to live is not just difficult; it is impossible. But Jesus hints at the solution following His injunction to the rich man: "With man this is impossible, but not with God; all things are possible with God" (Mark 10:27).

Humility

This propensity toward currying favor with God by our own effort didn't fade out with the Pharisees. In and around the beginning of the fifth century, there was a monk from Britain named Pelagius who struggled with the great St. Augustine's teaching on original sin and the need for grace. Augustine had essentially taught that the only way we can obey God is if God gives us the ability or grace to do so. Preredemption obedience to God was impossible because grace was not at work in us yet. Pelagius thought such logic was a corruption of the doctrine of free will: How could God command us to do something He knows is impossible for us to do? Where is the choice there? And if sin is all our will could choose—as a result of original sin—then shouldn't we be excused from sin?

Following that line of reasoning, Pelagius essentially proposed that if God requires it of us, we must be capable of it; we're simply not trying hard enough. Adam had a choice the same way we do;

there is no sin nature in us. We can choose righteousness, and so, we should.

It was in response to Pelagius that Augustine wrote his most important theological works. Augustine argued that—as I myself can attest—the "will is not always its own master, for it is clear that the will to will does not always have its way."[5] After the fall and before redemption, the best we can do is sin. All our choices, all our best efforts are still "filthy rags," or, as the euphemism suggests, used menstrual rags. Only by grace through faith in Jesus Christ— because of what He accomplished for us—are we justified, declared righteous before God. And once we are redeemed, the grace of God works in us, giving us both "the desire and the power to do what pleases him" (Phil. 2:13 NLT). Now I'm getting ahead of myself. The next chapter will deal more fully with the truth of God's amazing grace. For now, it is enough to say that Pelagius's teachings— Pelagianism—lasted only a few years before being rejected by the church. Paul's declaration in Romans was affirmed: "For all have sinned and fall short of the glory of God" (Rom. 3:23).

At the core of Pelagianism and our wrongheaded notions of pleasing God with our own good behavior is a certain pride. It may be a pride that says, *I deserved to be saved,* or, *I'm paying God back for saving me by behaving well,* or simply, *I'm a pretty good guy; I don't do anything to harm anybody; I'm sure I'll be in heaven.* Whether because of our own ignorance or from our overfamiliarity with the God of mercy and love, the falsehood of believing that we can please a holy God is really proof of our audacity. And if it is audacity that got us in trouble—just as it got the men of Beth-shemesh killed—then the only way out is humility.

And maybe the quickest path to humility is a swift kick in the head. Paul opted for that route when writing the Galatians. *The Message* phrases it this way:

> *Let me put this question to you: How did your new life
> begin? Was it by working your heads off to please God? Or
> was it by responding to God's Message to you? Are you going
> to continue this craziness? For only crazy people would think
> they could complete by their own efforts what was begun by
> God. If you weren't smart enough or strong enough to begin
> it, how do you suppose you could perfect it? Did you go
> through this whole painful learning process for nothing? It is
> not yet a total loss, but it certainly will be if you keep this up!*
> *(Gal. 3:2–4 MSG)*

Good people, good Christians, rotten people, fiendish sinners—we are all incapable of pleasing God, of satisfying the demands of His holiness.

We cannot stare at the law without the cover of blood.

We cannot handle what God demands of us without the grace He has provided for us. Thank God, the gospel does not end with our own inability. But without grasping this, what comes next won't make much sense.

DISCUSSION QUESTIONS:

1. Why is it so difficult to believe that our goodness will never be good enough?

2. How does the realization that it doesn't depend on your good effort bring relief?

3. In what ways do you identify with the Pharisees or Pelagius?

8. Holy

Question #3: Who Can Stand Before This God?

The AA meeting that Saturday morning in New York City was just another meeting for the people present. But for Andrew Delbanco, a Columbia University humanities professor who was traveling the country to research AA meetings, this gathering was the occasion of a powerful epiphany.

A sharply dressed young man began an exposition of his problems by explaining how all his troubles were really the result of being mistreated or betrayed by others. Delbanco, describing the scene, wrote, "His every gesture gave the impression of grievously wounded pride."[1] The young man was not only trying to justify himself; he was so full of resentment that he was vowing to avenge himself. As the young man was in the middle of his speech, a middle-aged black man with dark shades and dreadlocks leaned over to Delbanco and said, "I used to feel that way too, before I achieved low self-esteem." The phrase made such an impression on Delbanco that he wrote about it in his book *The Real American Dream: A Meditation on Hope.*

> *This was more than a good line. For me, it was the moment I understood in a new way the religion I had claimed to know something about. As the speaker bombarded us with phrases like "got to take control of my life," and "I've really got to believe in myself"—the man beside me took refuge in the old Calvinist doctrine that pride is the enemy of hope. What he meant by his joke about low self-esteem was that he learned no one can save himself by dint of his own efforts. He thought the speaker was still lost—lost in himself, but without knowing it.*[2]

We are tempted to make the same mistake. Every flaw or shortcoming is really someone else's fault. We would have been all right if not for what they did to us or said to us or didn't do or didn't say. At our core we believe that we are good, and that given the right environment, resources, and support, we can make it. But the road to freedom, for addicts and for the rest of us who sin in a less obviously compulsive way, begins with the same admission: I am powerless. I cannot change myself. I cannot make myself better. I can't starve my cravings enough to kill them. I can't please God on my own.

A God of Vengeance

Admitting that we cannot change ourselves is one step in the right direction. It involves a tremendous amount of humility. The next step is to understand the trouble we're in as a result. In other words, we've got to know that we can't save ourselves; then we need to know what it is that we can't save ourselves from. And to know that, we have to discover a truth about God—a truth that has been hidden or obscured by our culture.

I saw the new Batman movie, *The Dark Knight,* about a week ago. Though I was enthralled by the stunning storytelling, I came to a troubling realization at the movie's end: Batman doesn't kill the Joker. More accurately, Batman refuses to kill the Joker. It's against his code. This isn't new for Batman, neither is he alone in this Superhero Code of Ethics. To my best recollection, Superman and Spider-Man also refuse to kill even a villain. I've noticed this before, and I know the reason: They want to work within the city's system for punishing criminals rather than execute their own vigilante justice. But it never bothered me like it did in *The Dark Knight.* That's probably because there has never been a villain quite so evil, so demented, so fiendishly terrifying as Heath Ledger's Joker. In *WORLD Magazine*'s review, they point out that this villain is not based on any other human characterization of wickedness. This villain is based on Satan himself.[3] To me, a villain more evil than the worst human requires a hero greater than the best human. What's the point of a superhero if he won't do to our enemies what we cannot?

So what is with our superheroes? Why do they refuse to kill the bad guy?

The heroes of the Bible had no such problem. Young David ran to the battle with a sling in his hand and five smooth stones in his pouch, ready to take down the evil giant who had blasphemed the God of Israel. As if death were not enough, David lopped Goliath's head off in a display of triumph. Long before David's day, Joshua led the nation of Israel in complete and utter destruction of the pagan nations that opposed them. And before Joshua, Moses led Israel through the Red Sea on dry land only to have the waters come rushing back in over the Egyptians, drowning their army. In the Bible, the bad guys didn't just get caught; they got killed.

These passages make the modern man squeamish. We don't like violence, and we find it hard to believe in a God who employs such tactics, even against His enemies. We reference Jesus and His "love your enemies, turn the other cheek" speech as grounds for a new, nonviolent faith.

There is truth here: We no longer execute judgment against our own enemies. Human violence is not a means to righteousness, or as James wrote, "The wrath of man does not produce the righteousness of God" (James 1:20 NKJV). There is a civic system for meting out justice to the offender, and we ought to use such a system. Government, according to Romans 13, bears the sword for a reason, and those who do wrong should rightly fear the sword bearer. For example, in the case of rape, the victim ought not just forgive and let go, but forgive and report the perpetrator so that civil justice can be served and the community can be preserved. But vengeance and judgment are not ours as individuals to dish out.

Here is where many wrongfully make the leap of assuming that since Christianity advocates nonviolence against humans, then the Christian God must be a nonviolent God.

But if God is not violent, what then are we to make of the image of Jesus in the book of Revelation, a Jesus with fire in His eyes and a sword coming from His mouth, a Jesus who comes in justice to judge and make war, a Jesus who comes to "strike down the nations" (Rev. 19:11-16)? Jesus is no longer the Galilean peasant wandering the countryside. When we see Him next, He will come as King and Conqueror, the One who has vanquished sin and death and comes to bring justice to the earth. Heaven and earth will be remade, and His kingdom will come in totality. This is not a passive, nonviolent Jesus.

Miroslav Volf, a Yale theologian from Croatia who has witnessed the horrific violence in the Balkans, has an interesting perspective on why we ought to believe in a God of justice:

> *If God were not angry at injustice and deception and did not make a final end to violence—that God would not be worthy of worship.... The only means of prohibiting all recourse to violence by ourselves is to insist that violence is legitimate only when it comes from God.... My thesis that the practice of non-violence requires a belief in divine vengeance will be unpopular with many in the West.... [But] it takes the quiet of a suburban home for the birth of the thesis that human non-violence [results from the belief in] God's refusal to judge. In a sun-scorched land, soaked in the blood of the innocent, it will invariably die.*[4]

The reality is that we live in a world suffocating with evil. In the face of this reality, there is only one way humans can refrain from executing their own vigilante, violent justice and instead truly love their enemies: They need to believe and trust in a supremely powerful and personal God who is moved by our suffering and intends to act on our behalf by bringing an ultimate end to evil and evildoers one day.

But here's where we find the real rub: Believing in a God of justice and vengeance means believing in a God who cannot simply dismiss *my* assault on His honor and character, a God who must defend it and make someone pay. God's justice is not simply philosophical; it's personal. Every time I sin, I am spitting in God's face, insulting Him by my insistence on living apart from Him. I am saying He is not enough—not good enough, not powerful enough, not worthy enough—to have my devotion, dependence, and obedience. When I sin, I am in essence saying that God is not God. And if God is to be God, He cannot tolerate such mutiny and insult. It is an affront to His character. And I am the offender.

Trading Spaces

So what then? If God's justice requires Him to judge evil and punish sinners, aren't we all in trouble? Can't God simply forgive? After all, isn't He a God of love?

There is no such thing as simply forgiving, even at the human level. There is always a cost. When someone wrongs you, something is taken from you, a piece of you is gone. Sometimes it's something physical; more often it's something intangible, like your innocence, your childhood, your respect, your marriage. Fill in the blank. If you've been wronged, you are missing something you once had or should have had. That is why we instinctively feel like saying to the one who has wronged us, "You owe me!" Even our own justice system is based on the old Hebrew law of paying "an eye for an eye"—i.e., making the punishment fit the crime, requiring restitution and replacement where possible.

We have wronged God and He—because He is just—cannot simply forgive us. Someone must bear the cost.

Back to our story of the ark.

The ark of the covenant had finally been returned to Israel on an oxcart from the Philistines. The people were overjoyed at the sight. There were sacrifices and songs of joy. But then the tragic happened unexpectedly.

The men of Beth-shemesh opened the cover of the ark and looked in at the law without the cover of blood, and they were struck dead. The people of Beth-shemesh, seeing seventy of their men suddenly slain because of the wrath of God, cried out, "Who can stand in the presence of the LORD, this holy God?" (1 Sam. 6:20).

This same question can lead us on the road to salvation. In this question is a truth we have missed: God is holy.

You see, God's sense of justice is rooted in His holiness. To properly understand His justice, we have to recognize His holiness. To say that God is holy is to say that God is far removed from us not just by degree but also in kind. He is not the top of the spectrum on which we lie near the bottom; He is on a spectrum wholly different than ours. He is, literally, in a league of His own. That is enough to require a mediator. But to make matters worse, we are fallen, sinful creatures. Adam was the first to attempt a life apart from God, to try to live as God instead of with Him. That sin has been passed on to the rest of us, embedded in our very nature. But we are not passive in this. By our own actions we confirm our sinfulness and our desire to rebel and live apart from God. By our own choice, we have become enemies of God.

This presents a problem on a cosmic scale. Throughout the Old Testament, there are hints and references to a "cup of wrath" waiting to be poured out in judgment on the nations.

Psalm 75:8 says, "In the hand of the LORD is a cup full of foaming wine mixed with spices; he pours it out, and all the wicked of the earth drink it down to its very dregs."

In a prophecy against Judah, Ezekiel warns, "This is what the Sovereign LORD says: 'You will drink your sister's cup, a cup large and deep; it will bring scorn and derision, for it holds so much. You will be filled with drunkenness and sorrow, the cup of ruin and desolation, the cup of your sister Samaria. You will drink it and drain it dry; you will dash it to pieces and tear your breasts. I have spoken,' declares the Sovereign LORD" (Ez. 23:32–34).

The book of Revelation gives a glimpse into the final judgment that awaits:

> *A third angel followed them and said in a loud voice: "If anyone worships the beast and his image and receives his mark on the forehead or on the hand, he, too, will drink of the wine of God's fury, which has been poured full strength into the cup of his wrath. He will be tormented with burning sulfur in the presence of the holy angels and of the Lamb.*

*And the smoke of their torment rises for ever and ever. There
is no rest day or night for those who worship the beast and
his image, or for anyone who receives the mark of his name."
(Rev. 14:9–11)*

A cup in Scripture is symbolic of a person's lot or portion in life.
To be an enemy of God is to deserve the cup of wrath, the cup of
ruin, sorrow, and destruction. It is our lot, and our coming portion
forever.

But God did the unthinkable. He sent His own Son—who is
God forever—to come to earth and drink the cup that was meant
for us. It is interesting that when James and John asked—or more
accurately, when their mother asked!—if they could sit at the right
and left hand of Jesus, He said to them, "Can you drink the cup I am
going to drink?" (Matt. 20:22).

Later, in the garden of Gethsemane, Jesus prayed, "My Father,
if it is possible, may this cup be taken from me. Yet not as I will, but
as you will" (Matt. 26:39). And a second time in the garden, "My
Father, if it is not possible for this cup to be taken away unless I drink
it, may your will be done" (Matt. 26:42).

Let this cup pass. What was Jesus' portion? The cup of wrath.
The cup of ruin, sorrow, and destruction. It was a heavy lot to have,
yet it was one only Jesus could bear. Only God could satisfy the
honor of God. Only God could be holy enough to take on the sin of
all the world and with it all the destruction due to us. Jesus took for
us the full blow, the full force of God's wrath so that we no longer
have to taste God's judgment.

Instead, our cup, our lot, is now the cup of blessing, symbolized in the cup of Communion. The apostle Paul wrote, "The cup of blessing that we bless, is it not a participation in the blood of Christ? The bread that we break, is it not a participation in the body of Christ?" (1 Cor. 10:16 ESV).

We switched cups! Jesus drank the cup of God's wrath instead of us so that we can drink the cup of blessing. The cup of blessing is ours because of the new covenant. John Stott words the miraculous reversal of roles this way:

> *The essence of sin is we human beings substituting ourselves for God, while the essence of salvation is God substituting himself for us. We ... put ourselves where only God deserves to be; God ... puts himself where we deserve to be.*[5]

Love So Amazing

What kind of love is this, that God, at great cost to Himself, would make Himself pay for what we owed Him? In Christ, God came to do for us what we could not. This is amazing grace.

How should we respond? The tendency is to try to repay God with our good behavior, to show Him His death was worth it, that we are worth it. But here again, our goodness could not be good enough.

C. S. Lewis, knowing our propensity to try to repay God for His grace or to give God our obedience as a sort of "paying taxes" to the One who gave us the benefits we enjoy, wrote about the conventional approach to morality and how the Christian's approach is in reality and should be in practice.

But we are hoping all the time that when all the demands [of morality and society] have been met, the poor natural self will still have some chance, some time, to get on with its own life and do what it likes. In fact, we are very like an honest man paying his taxes. He pays them all right, but he does hope that there will be enough left over for him to live on....

The Christian way is different: harder and easier. Christ says, "Give me All. I don't want so much of your time and so much of your money and so much of your work: I want you. I have not come to torment your natural self, but to kill it.... Hand over the whole natural self, all the desires which you think are innocent as well as the ones you think wicked—the whole outfit. I will give you a new self instead. In fact, I will give you Myself: my own will shall become yours."[6]

Lewis continues to point out how what seems impossible is made possible because of Christ and what seemed possible is in reality impossible:

The terrible thing, the almost impossible thing, is to hand over your whole self—all your wishes and precautions—to Christ. But it is far easier than what we are all trying to do instead. For what we are trying to do is to remain what we call "ourselves", to keep personal happiness as our great aim in life, and yet at the same time be "good". We are all trying to let our mind and heart go their own way—centered on money or pleasure or ambition—and hoping, in spite of this, to behave honestly and chastely and humbly. And that is exactly what

Christ warned us you could not do. If I am a grass field that contains nothing but grass seed, I cannot produce wheat. Cutting the grass may keep it short: but I shall still produce grass and no wheat. If I want to produce wheat ... I must be ploughed up and re-sown.[7]

Our response to God is not to try to repay or try to filter our behavior enough to become better. It is to surrender, completely and fully, out of love for Him. The only way to respond to such lavish love from God is love in return—the kind of love that makes us give ourselves fully to Him.

Timothy Keller is the pastor of a booming Presbyterian church located in the heart of Manhattan. He recounts the story of a woman who had been coming to the church and was getting scared of the gospel of grace she was discovering. She had been more familiar with the kind of Christianity that taught that if we are good enough, God will accept us. But this new understanding of a God who paid the price Himself and accepts us because of what *He* has done was unnerving. Asked to explain, she said:

If I was saved by my good works then there would be a limit to what God could ask of me or put me through. I would be like a taxpayer with "rights"—I would have done my duty and now I would deserve a certain quality of life. But if I am a sinner saved by sheer grace—then there's nothing he cannot ask of me.[8]

How true.

The Difference

Back at the small group my wife and I attended with several older, wiser couples we admired, things started to get spicy. After a few rounds of lamenting our "poor Christian witness" and the negative effect it has had on our attempts at evangelism, my wife decided to speak up. In essence, she said, "What if our good behavior is not really the good news?" Several approving nods. A few quizzical looks. Never one to leave my thoughts unsaid, I rushed through the door my wife had gently opened.

"Christianity is not first about becoming better people; it is about becoming alive! Behavior modification can be achieved through a number of different means." At this point, I glanced over at the man in his sixties who had spent the last several decades of his life as a licensed counselor. He nodded. I took that as permission to proceed. I referenced C. S. Lewis's famous chapter in *Mere Christianity*, "Nice People or New Men." A man may be better behaved than a Christian because of his socioeconomic background or family upbringing—and because the Christian may have been rescued out of a life of drugs and self-destruction. "The good news isn't that we simply behave better; the good news is twofold: that we have been forgiven, and that our hearts have been made alive to God!" I had taken the floor and was enjoying it just a little too much. But I wasn't about to stop now. I then committed the cardinal sin for a young pastor among a group of wiser elders: I quoted myself! Referencing a sermon I had just given at theMILL, our college and twentysomethings service, I mentioned the illustration of a perfectly shaped mannequin versus a living man with a not-so-chiseled physique. "Sure, the mannequin may look better, but he's not alive!"

I noticed they were now smiling at me like a parent smiles at a two-year-old's dance routine. It was not great, but boy, was it heartwarming to watch. Of course they were familiar with Lewis's argument and his—yes, Lewis's—mannequin analogy. They were gracious in their agreement. Then the statesmanlike counselor in our small group, after letting me rant, finally spoke. He told of how he had seen far too many people in his office glad to be alive in Christ yet still intent on screwing up their lives! In other words, yes, they were new and alive, but they had refused to allow that grace that had made them new also make them different.

As Christians, we understand what our gospel is all about, at least in theory. But we run into an old accusation against Christians by those who know little of its doctrine: How can those who cling to such high moral standards so frequently fail by those same standards? The answer is layered. Timothy Keller, in his thorough yet accessible book *The Reason for God*, takes the issue head-on:

> *If Christianity is all it claims to be, shouldn't Christians on the whole be much better people than everyone else?*
>
> *This assumption is based on a mistaken belief concerning what Christianity actually teaches about itself. Christian theology has taught what is known as common grace.... This means that no matter who performs it, every act of goodness, wisdom, justice, and beauty is empowered by God....*
>
> *Christian theology also speaks of the seriously flawed character of real Christians. A central message of the Bible is that*

we can only have relationship with God by sheer grace.... The mistaken belief that a person must "clean up" his or her own life in order to merit God's presence is not Christianity. This means, though, that the church will be filled with immature and broken people who still have a long way to go emotionally, morally, and spiritually.[9]

This is helpful to remember. But at our group, we were still wrestling with the tension of Christianity not being centrally about good behavior, but still being about a visible transformation. Yet, why is that still so hard to see? Here again, Keller is helpful. Bringing the point to bear on real life with laserlike precision, he writes:

Now imagine that someone with a very broken past becomes a Christian and her character improves significantly over what it was. Nevertheless, she still may be less secure and self-disciplined than someone who is so well adjusted that she feels no particular need for religious affiliation at all. Suppose you meet both of these women the same week. Unless you know the starting points and life journeys of each woman, you could easily conclude that Christianity isn't worth much, and that Christians are inconsistent with their own high standards.[10]

Christianity *is* about transformation. The old bumper sticker that reads, "Christians aren't perfect, just forgiven" gets it only half-right. We are forgiven. But we are also new. We are alive. We are

different. We now have the ability to obey God, whereas before our
only option was to sin.

Two applications leap out to me from this powerful truth.
First, we cannot curse the darkness for being dark. Sinning is all a
sinner knows to do and all a sinner is able to do. It does no good for
the church to beg the world—or berate the world or beat the world
or legislate the world—into better behavior. Sin is the best they
can ever do. Secondly, it is Christians who now have a different
power at work in us. We now have the option not to "let sin reign"
(Rom. 6:12); we now have the ability to "walk in the Spirit" so we
will "not fulfill the lust of the flesh" (Gal. 5:16 NKJV). If anything,
we should be tougher on sin in the church than we are on sin by
the nonbeliever. Instead, we spend our time and energy picketing
Hollywood and protesting sinners, while we let fallen Christians
off the hook in the name of grace. In the name of grace, we should
call Christians to a higher standard because Christ is now at work
in them. This is exactly the approach the apostle Paul took when
he recommended not even eating with a believer who persisted in
conscious, blatant sin. It is also seen in the way he wrote to the
churches, urging them to "walk worthy of [their] calling" (Eph.
4:1 NKJV).

By grace, God came from heaven and suffered for our disobedience; by grace, in Christ, we are now obedient sons and daughters.
But grace has no intention of stopping there. Grace intends to conquer our hearts so fully that we surrender and learn obedience in our
own actions. Grace, as we said in the last chapter, is God working in
us both "to will and to do for His good pleasure" (Phil. 2:13 NKJV).
Grace doesn't make our obedience irrelevant; it makes our obedience

possible. Without grace, we have no strength, no option to do what God has required of us. With grace—with God—all things are possible. Christ in us has become the hope of glory. This is the truth about amazing grace.

DISCUSSION QUESTIONS:

1. How does understanding God's holiness, justice, and wrath help you understand or appreciate His grace?

2. In what ways have you tried to "repay God" for His salvation and forgiveness?

3. How does your view of grace—as forgiveness and the desire and power to do God's will—change your view of transformation? How is grace working in you?

9. Carts

Rumor #4: God Prefers Specialists.

People start acting funny whenever they find out I'm a pastor. Sometimes they give me a look that says, *Really? Seriously? You? Where's your collar?* Or, *Aren't you a little young for that?* But other times it makes them squirm a little. On an airplane, the mere mention of my occupation can be a conversation killer. "Oh. Hmm. Interesting." And just like that, the airplane information card seems more interesting.

The best response is from my wife's extended family. Ever since I've been in the family, I'm usually the one that prays for Thanksgiving or Christmas meal—actually, I think I get asked to pray for just about every meal! If there's a question about God or the Bible or church, they consult me. If there's a family event like a wedding, I get to share a song or a Scripture or even officiate. It is a strange and delightful honor to be a sort of resident "God expert."

Even in my own city, people easily believe that since I'm a pastor or I work at the church or I'm on the platform, then I must know God better than they do. There's nothing inherently wrong with that. After all, those who are in ministry leadership are held to a higher standard. They are the ones who should be devoting themselves "to prayer and to the ministry of the word" (Acts 6:4 NASB). We can all benefit from those who have been walking with the Lord longer than we have.

Where this becomes dangerous, though, is when a pastor or a leader or even an author becomes a substitute for our relationship with God, when we start to excuse ourselves of the duty and delight of knowing God simply because we aren't in the "ministry." I have a friend who thinks that every time a conversation turns spiritual, it's only because so many in our friend group work at the church. He might be right, but there is a prevalent and less innocuous way of explaining why pastors talk about the Bible and God so much. It's the underlying belief that pastors read their Bibles or know how to pray or talk to God or hear His voice because they're pastors! They're supposed to know about their own field. It's as if people think a pastor knowing about the Bible is akin to a stockbroker knowing about funds and market forces or a realtor knowing about houses and neighborhoods. We pastors read our Bibles just as businesspeople read the *Wall Street Journal:* It's just part of our job.

And while it certainly is part of a pastor's "job" to study the Scriptures, the average Christian has begun to think that knowing

God is almost exclusively the pastor's job, set in contrast to the layperson's job of making money. It's kind of a warped way of looking at the body of Christ: *You know, we all have our roles, and some make the money, others seek to know God.*

Of course, we wouldn't really word it like that. We just kind of live like that. And it makes sense in today's society. We have experts for everything we need in life. We have a CPA who does our taxes, a doctor who tells us what pills to take, and a counselor who shows us where our relationships are dysfunctional. (By the way, I have benefited from and am a fan of all these services.) But these days, there are also God experts. They are people whose job it is to do the hard work of knowing God and then condense it for us in a few bullet points in church every Sunday.

The truth is this desire to have someone or something else do the heavy lifting of a real relationship with God is not a new impulse. It's seen right here in 1 Chronicles, where our story of the ark picks up.

Tragic Revival

After that devastating day in Beth-shemesh, when seventy men were struck dead for looking in the ark, the ark was moved to another Israelite town, Kiriath Jearim. At least twenty years had gone by and the people of Israel asked for a king. God gave them Saul. There was no appearance of the ark during the reign of Saul, something that might indicate his own lack of devotion to God or passion for His presence. Eventually, Saul died in battle, and David, who had been anointed king some fifteen years or so earlier, was finally crowned as king, coronated in a short time by all twelve tribes.

The first thing David wanted to do was to bring the ark back to Jerusalem, the center of activity and the site of his palace.

> *David conferred with each of his officers, the commanders of thousands and commanders of hundreds. He then said to the whole assembly of Israel, "If it seems good to you and if it is the will of the LORD our God, let us send word far and wide to the rest of our brothers throughout the territories of Israel, and also to the priests and Levites who are with them in their towns and pasturelands, to come and join us. Let us bring the ark of our God back to us, for we did not inquire of it during the reign of Saul." The whole assembly agreed to do this, because it seemed right to all the people. (1 Chron. 13:1–4)*

The ark had not been part of Israel's national life for years. For the entire duration of Saul's reign, no one had inquired of it, no one had encountered God at the ark; it had been ignored. In a very real sense, *God* had been ignored. And now David wanted to bring God back. It was an incredible vision. David's speech was more inspirational that day than JFK's "Ask not what your country can do for you" speech several decades ago or Obama's "Yes, We Can" acceptance speech in 2008. This was a moment of epic national significance.

> *They moved the ark of God from Abinadab's house on a new cart, with Uzzah and Ahio guiding it. David and all the Israelites were celebrating with all their might before God, with songs and with harps, lyres, tambourines, cymbals and trumpets. (1 Chron. 13:7–8)*

This was a major celebration. Think Macy's Thanksgiving Day
Parade meets bicentennial Fourth of July meets New Year's Eve 1999.
It was a massive event. But something went horribly wrong.

When they came to the threshing floor of Kidon, Uzzah
reached out his hand to steady the ark, because the oxen
stumbled. The LORD's anger burned against Uzzah, and he
struck him down because he had put his hand on the ark. So
he died there before God. (1 Chron. 13:9–10)

What started with singing ended with weeping; what began as a
revival ended as a funeral.

No Carts Allowed

Once again, Israel is faced with a "what the heck?" moment, an
opportunity either to curse God and walk away, or wrestle with God
and find His face. What made David a great king was his repeated
choice of the latter. It didn't take David long to recognize his mistake. Addressing the priests about three months later, David said, "It
was because you, the Levites, did not bring it up the first time that
the LORD our God broke out in anger against us. We did not inquire
of him about how to do it in the prescribed way" (1 Chron. 15:13).

What was the prescribed way? The ark was to be carried by the
Levites, using the poles that ran on either side.

So the priests and Levites consecrated themselves in order
to bring up the ark of the LORD, the God of Israel. And the

Levites carried the ark of God with the poles on their shoulders, as Moses had commanded in accordance with the word of the LORD. (1 Chron. 15:14–15)

Why had they not done that the first time? Where did the idea of a cart come from?

The only other time the Bible records the ark being moved around on a cart driven by oxen was when the Philistines had done it decades earlier in their desperate attempt to rid themselves of Israel's God. It seems likely that when the time came to bring the ark to Jerusalem, someone remembered that day. I imagine the scene going something like this:

Levite 1: Hey, King David wants to bring the ark to Jerusalem.

Levite crowd: (Cheers) Fantastic! What a great idea!

Levite 2: You know, I have a thought …

Levite 1: Yes?

Levite 2: Oh, never mind … it's probably too radical …

Levite 1: No, what is it?

Levite 2: Well … it's just that, there are these wonderful things nowadays called "carts" … and … well … they work so wonderfully …

Levite 1: You don't mean …?

Levite 2: I know, I know … too crazy, right?

Levite 3: Um … if I may … the Philistines used a cart years ago when they were returning the ark …

Levite 1: (nods in agreement) Yes, yes. I remember! My grandfather was there at Beth-shemesh!

Levite 2: Well, that's what I mean. It worked for them … and God didn't judge them.

Levite 1: Yeah …

Levite 2: It's so much easier … I mean, we're not getting any younger and to carry the heavy box covered in gold all the way …

Levite 3: He's right. God won't mind. It's progress, a tribute to a more modern way of approaching God …

Levite 2: Not to mention much more efficient. This is going to make things much easier.

Levite 1: Okay. Sounds like we agree. Prepare the cart!

Obviously, I'm taking liberties with my imagination. But here's what we do know from Scripture: Operation "Bring the ark to Jerusalem" went awry long before Uzzah reached out his hand to steady the ark from falling. It had nothing to do with clumsy cows who happened to stumble. It had everything to do with the decision to place the ark on a cart driven by oxen instead of on the shoulders of priests, where it was meant to be in the first place.

For us, in the New Testament era, every believer in Christ is called a "priest"; we are the new Levites. We are the ones God, in His amazing grace, called into relationship with Him, at great cost to His Son. Yet we are not too different from the Levites of David's day. We all too often abdicate our role as priest and defer to the more efficient, more progressive approach of using carts.

A cart is anything we use to "carry God" for us; it is the shortcuts we attempt and the God experts we prefer, the people, places, conferences, events, songs, styles, churches—fill in the blank—that we rely on to bring God to us in a quick, easy, but devastatingly impersonal way. What's worse than our reliance on them is our belief that God actually prefers them.

This is the fourth and last rumor about God: God prefers specialists.

Second-Class Christians

Though this is the last rumor addressed in this book, it is in reality the first rumor that leads us to a secondhand Jesus. This is the rumor to begin all rumors, the mother of all half-truths, misinformation, and a faith we hold at arm's length. Once we believe that God prefers specialists, that there is a distinction between pastors and "normal Christians," then we have forfeited our privilege, declined the divine invitation, and doomed ourselves to living by "crumbs of rumor."

It is very possible that this notion of God experts originated from an ancient sort of class division within the church.

In the late fourth century, when Christianity became the official religion of the Roman Empire, Christians everywhere rejoiced. Surely this was the triumph of the gospel that they had been hoping for. In less than one generation, Christians went from being persecuted in arenas to being celebrated in official halls. The same imperial basilicas where Christians were tried as criminals for their faith became the hallowed halls of Christian worship. From a marginalized religion that was viewed with suspicion, questioned as a new faith, and criticized for the belief in an unseen God, Christianity became all the rage.

But the rise of Christianity wasn't the result of Constantine's conversion or Theodisius I's edict. By sociologist Rodney Stark's analysis, those marquee events were results of a faith already spreading like wildfire. In fact, it was this among other discoveries that led Stark, an unbeliever when he began his study of the rise of Christianity, to his own conversion.

Still, Christianity was tested most not in the era of persecution but in the centuries of favor and political dominance that followed. It was these first decades of newfound influence that gave occasion to doubt the legitimacy of a person's conversion. After all, who could be sure if a person was converting merely for social reasons rather than out of genuine spiritual conviction? It makes sense, then, that in this era, the process of "being saved" became far more involved. The *Apostolic Tradition* provides detail of the conversion process in fourth-century Rome. It began with the *catechumenate*, an extended period of "hearing the Word" that could last as long as three years. Each year, candidates were chosen from this group to advance to the next round, where they would undergo "further examination of life style and daily exorcism."[1] Finally, after intense preparation and examination, the candidate would be baptized—likely on Easter morning—anointed with oil, and blessed by the bishop. The new convert could now give the kiss of peace for the first time and partake of his first Communion. It seems like it might be easier to become the next American Idol than to have become a Christian in the fourth century.

It was also during this era that monasticism first began to appear. Wrestling to find ways to show true devotion to Christ in the midst of a church that was becoming increasingly secular, the first monastics made radical breaks with society, voluntarily taking vows that went above and beyond the call of Christian "duty." In the previous era, a person displayed his commitment to Christ through willingness to die for his faith. In an age where that was no longer possible, when the most powerful man on earth—the emperor himself—was a professing Christian, how could you prove the depth of your love and commitment? James White, professor at Notre Dame, postulates that monasticism was just the answer. In his book *A Brief History of Christian Worship,* he writes, "Monasticism replaced martyrdom"[2]

Monasticism helped answer a host of difficult questions and contradictions a sincere and devout believer might have faced.

- *How do you worship a Christ who suffered while being yourself part of a church that prospers?*
- *How do you demonstrate holiness in a culture of Christianity that is increasingly worldly?*
- *How do you live separately from the world when the church is the center of society?*
- *How do you cling to a Christ who had little or no earthly possessions while living in a city where the church is the largest and most prominent building?*
- *How do you anticipate a kingdom not of this world when the kingdom of this world confesses allegiance to your same King?*

These questions have surfaced again as real issues that every believer must wrestle with. Part of the answer for many believers in the fourth century and centuries to follow was monasticism. The monastic movement is responsible for much good, both for the society around it and for the church at large. Out of many of these orders came beautiful art and song. These amazing men and women practiced the habits of discipline and service to near perfection.

But monasticism also had an unintended consequence. It created a sort of class division among Christians. For example, many of the monastic orders had cycles that required prayer several times a day. In the mid-fourth century, Basil, the bishop of Caesarea, drew up a set of monastic rules to regulate urban monastic groups, outlining eight daily occasions for prayer. That's roughly every three hours—or about as often as a parent feeds a new baby for the first wonderfully grueling months. The message unintentionally sent and heard was that, if you couldn't commit to prayer eight times a day, then you had better just leave it to the professionals. In a largely agrarian society, common people could not afford the luxury of that kind of devotion. Professor White's assessment and analogy is helpful:

> *What was happening as the popular religion of the people's office slipped out of sight was that daily prayer had become professionalized with the monks taking it over. Eventually local clergy followed monastic practices but left little prayer of a public nature for ordinary folk. The whole approach had become that of an athletic discipline, well suited to the needs of those intent on meditation and contemplation, but hardly suited for those raising a family.*[3]

For the nonmonastics, they had to make their peace with being a second-class Christian.

A New Monasticism

Most Christians we know don't commit themselves to monasteries or nunneries. But the spirit of the monastic age is alive even among the fiercest nontraditionalists. I know Christians who think the word "tradition" is tantamount to spiritual death yet are themselves part of a tradition that gives them a feeling of superiority over the average churchgoing Susie. It's the conference circuit. These days the ones who watch more Christian TV, attend more Christian conferences—preferably of the supernatural or prophetic variety—or go to church every time the doors are open are the neomonastics. These are the fervent ones who show their commitment to Christ by their frequent attendance of Christian gatherings. There is nothing necessarily wrong with that. Yet this in our day, like monasticism centuries ago, is an occasion for creating class division within the church. Those who do more "Christian things" or go to more Christian events come to be viewed as the "God experts," the "spiritual specialists," and those who don't, well, are practically backslidden.

The truth is, both groups—the ones who fill their lives with special Christian activities and those who can't or don't—have equal access to God. And both are equally prone to relying on "carts."

The ones who live a more secular life, who work out in the so-called real world, tend to excuse themselves of any spiritual duty or effort because "we ought to leave all that God stuff to the pros." Ah, yes. God professionals. The fact that there are those who are in vocational ministry—and I am numbered among those—can just complicate things further. It's a common mistake to think that someone who works at church is a sort of professional Christian. It's sort of like cooking. All of us can throw together our favorite recipes, but we don't do it for a living. We're not *that* good. A professional chef is an amazing cook. But when it comes to knowing God, not only do we have equal access to God, we have an equal shot at knowing Him as well as the next guy. A pastor or a person in vocational ministry is in that role because of their function, not because of their relationship or potential relationship with God. In other words, the fivefold ministry—the designations of apostle, prophet, evangelist, pastor, and teacher—has everything to do with a role or functional office within the body of Christ and nothing to do with their access to God. Every believer has equal access to God and equal potential to know Him. To say it plainly: You can know God just as well as a pastor, prophet, evangelist, teacher, or apostle. So neither the pastor nor the conference junkie should be used as a sort of cart.

But the so-called insiders, those in vocational ministry or those who fill their time with church activities and Christian events, tend to have carts of their own as well.

I can attest to this firsthand. I began this book by telling you about the event that jolted me to attention and attentiveness in my spiritual walk. I was coasting—which is another way of saying I had begun to rely on a few carts to carry my spiritual life for me. For instance, it had been enough for me to know that there were others who were praying diligently every morning. I could afford to be irregular. It was excusable that my study of the Bible was stale and inconsistent; I knew others were reading commentaries and devoting time to study. It was okay that my time to listen to God was hurried and squeezed in during drive time between appointments. Someone else was listening for vision and direction. That's good enough, right?

Wrong. The scandal of November 2006 was a resounding message, just as Uzzah's death had been a signal to King David. My cart had slipped and was heading for the mud. But the real problem was not that my cart had slipped but that I, like Uzzah, had been relying on a cart in the first place. God dwells in human hearts, not man-made carts. God didn't want me leaning completely on someone else's knowledge of Him; He didn't want me coasting, finding shortcuts for knowing Him. He wanted me to do the carrying, the heavy lifting, the hard and delightfully glorious work of knowing Him.

It's not so much about the new things I'm doing, though there are some new habits I'm trying to form. It is more about a privilege I'm not ignoring, an invitation I'm not declining. God wants contact with me. And I can no longer forfeit that joy.

What About the Experts?

What can be intimidating is the knowledge gap between regular churchgoing folks and the seminary grad. People tend to feel that since they don't know much about Hebrew or Greek or Jewish culture and can't always properly exegete a text, they must resign themselves to being a second-class Christian with a secondhand knowledge of God. It is better to use the cart of the scholar. But there is confusion here between knowledge and access or relationship. A scholar will have more knowledge about the text and about God and about doctrine. But a scholar does not have more *access* to God than you do. Furthermore, a scholar may have knowledge without having relationship with the living God. Scan the faculties of many prestigious, once-great seminaries, and you'll find learned men and women who are hollow on the inside. To some degree, this was the case for even the great Henri Nouwen before he left Harvard.

The opposite but equal error is to then dismiss all scholarly work or diligent research and reduce all of the Christian life to what "the Holy Spirit shows me from the Bible." This is simply foolishness. The two are not mutually exclusive, though they are often excluded from each other. There are many wonderful scholars whose hearts burn with passion and relationship with a living Christ. Their works fill my bookshelf. My point here about using carts and relying on God experts is not that we should never devote ourselves to study or consult commentaries and dictionaries and Bible encyclopedias. My point is that the one with more knowledge does not have more access. We all have equal access and should never forfeit our privilege of having relationship with God. In pursuit of that relationship with God we will often need to consult scholars and experts for textual and contextual help when it comes to gaining knowledge about the Bible or the background or the language or even the doctrine—but we never need them in our knowledge of God personally or relationally. We don't need someone to talk to God for us; we can come ourselves. We don't need someone to worship for us; we can bring our lives, broken as they are. We have Jesus who has made the way. The possession of knowledge is not a division of class in the kingdom of God. We are all sons and daughters.

God does not prefer specialists; He passionately desires *you.*

DISCUSSION QUESTIONS:

1. What or who are some "carts" in your life?

2. How do you think the monastic impulse is seen among Christians today?

3. What place should pastors, leaders, resources, and study tools hold in our lives?

10. Contact

Question #4: How Can God Come to Me?

So far, every time something has gone wrong with the ark, there has been a question echoing in the wake. Each question has been a clue for us, helping us trade in a rumor of God for a faith more rich and true.

"Where has the glory gone?" they asked after the ark was captured by the Philistines, hinting that God is the only thing worth having in the first place. He won't be used as a genie for our wants. He is not a means to an end; He is the greatest end in and of Himself.

"How can we get rid of this God?" the frustrated Philistines exclaimed after their god had been disgraced and their people had been covered in boils and tumors. The question points to the

fact that you can't have both God and idols. So the Philistines—
mystifyingly—chose to get rid of the one true God.

"Who is able to stand in the presence of the Lord, this holy
God?" the people of Beth-shemesh cried after seventy men were
struck down for looking at the law without the cover of blood.
The question reveals the universal unworthiness of humanity and
infinite supremacy of God in His holiness. Yet the cover of blood
was what they removed, and it is what we ignore when we imagine
that we can please God on our own. We must always depend on the
grace of God in Christ Jesus.

David's question, the one he asks after Uzzah died and before
the ark was sent to Obed-Edom's house, has a different texture
than the others. It still carried an air of desperation, frustration, and
even fear. But there was something different about it. Somewhere
in the midst of darker emotions was the unmistakable presence of
desire and longing for God.

David was afraid of the LORD that day and said, "How can
the ark of the LORD ever come to me?" (2 Sam. 6:9)

Even in confusion and fear, David's desire for God was unswerving. Undeterred by this wrong turn, David let his "what the heck?"
moment drive him to discover the error of his approach. Like Job,
he had lived by rumors, following a pattern for handling God that he
had seen someone else use—in David's case, using a cart like the
Philistines had—an approach that he knew was deficient. And like
Job, he refused to walk away. He engaged God, wrestling like Jacob
until he saw Him face-to-face. In the three other stories of the ark,

the ark was taken away or sent away. Here, David wants to find a way to bring God back, to have Him near. He is not content with a distant God.

How can God come to me?

As with the other three questions, this one contains a hint at the truth about God: He wants to be with us. He does not prefer efficient, expedient shortcuts or God experts; He wants us. The way the ark was designed suggests this. The poles on either side make it obvious that the best way to transport it was to carry it. It is a statement that resonates today: God wants contact with you and wants you to have contact with Him.

David knew that and would have it no other way.

In the Old Testament, the "contact" had to be mediated by a high priest. Even the ark had to be carried by Levites, and even then, they couldn't exactly touch the ark itself, only the poles. But for believers in Christ, we are all called priests, offering the living sacrifices of our own lives. Moreover, we are now the temple. We are now the new dwelling place of God.

Oh, To Be a Worship Pastor

But what exactly does that look like? How does that work in the *real* world?

From time to time, when good, God-loving, churchgoing Christians find out that I don't just volunteer on the worship team but that worship leading is part of my job description and that I get to work with other amazing worship leaders and songwriters and that we all have offices together, they tilt their heads back, drop their jaws, and gasp with sanctified envy—"Oh, how wonderful it must be! I can't imagine the times in the presence of God you must have together! Do you worship all day long? Wow!" Then they shake their heads in amazement and say, "I wish I could have your job. You are truly blessed!"

Yes, I do feel blessed. No, we do not spend time worshipping together all day long or even for part of the day. Funny as the thought may seem, when most of us think about what it means to "carry the presence of God," we usually think about worship music. And as a worship songwriter and worship leader, I completely understand that. Many of our dramatic encounters with God occur in the context of a corporate worship service. Or even if our tearful God-moments happen when we're alone, there is usually a soundtrack of worship music. So, naturally, when we think of being a carrier of God's presence, our minds turn to ways to surround ourselves with worship music. Music is an incredibly powerful tool and has long been hailed as the queen of the arts. It has a way of arresting our hearts, capturing our imagination, and making us stand in awe, shout with thanksgiving, dance with joy, and weep with sorrow. The ancient Hebrews knew this power and used it to its fullest capacity in their worship of Yahweh. Not only can music move us in uniquely powerful ways, it also may be the most powerful vehicle for self-expression. It makes sense then that the heavenly scenes in John's revelation are full of music and singing as saints, elders, and living creatures respond to the brilliance of God's glory.

Yet despite music's inherent power and pivotal role in our private and corporate worship, it is not the magic elixir in our quest to become carriers of God's presence. Our journey begins with a decision to accept the divine offer. But what follows is every bit as important. The word the Bible uses for the process that follows this choice is "sanctification."

Set Apart

In the Old Testament, when the people of God were about to be part of something significant, something epic and divine, they were commanded to "sanctify" themselves. For example, before Joshua led the children of Israel miraculously across the Jordan River, he said to the people, "Sanctify yourselves, for tomorrow the LORD will do wonders among you" (Josh. 3:5 NKJV).

In our final story of the ark for this book, David gives a similar command. After David prepared a place for the ark in Jerusalem, he announced how the ark was supposed to be transported— according to God's design. "Then David said, 'No one may carry the ark of God but the Levites, for the LORD has chosen them to carry the ark of God and to minister before Him forever'" (1 Chron. 15:2 NKJV).

He then gathered the whole nation together along with the descendants of Aaron, the first high priest, and all the Levites, and said to them:

> *You are the heads of the fathers' houses of the Levites; sanctify yourselves, you and your brethren, that you may bring up the ark of the LORD God of Israel to the place I have prepared for it. For because you did not do it the first time, the LORD our*

God broke out against us, because we did not consult Him
about the proper order. (1 Chron. 15:12–13 NKJV)

The idea of sanctification is simply to be "set apart," to be separated from something in order to be set apart for something. In some ways, it carries the idea of a woman who is betrothed to a man—or in our language, engaged. She is "separated" from all other guys and "set apart" for the one to whom she has promised her love and life. She is no longer available.

In the New Testament, the word "sanctification" is used to describe the work of the Holy Spirit in the life of the believer, making her more like Christ. To understand it in context of God's saving work, it can be helpful to recognize three "tenses" in which salvation occurs. When we believe in Christ and trust Him completely for our salvation, we receive His grace and are justified. We are declared to be righteous on the basis of Christ's righteousness and what He has done by taking our place. This can be described as the "past tense" part of our salvation. "For it is by grace you have been saved, through faith—and this not from yourselves, it is the gift of God" (Eph. 2:8). This is our being saved from the penalty of sin on the basis of faith in Christ.

But the New Testament also describes our salvation in the present continuous tense. "For the message of the cross is foolishness to those who are perishing, but to us who are being saved it is the power of God" (1 Cor. 1:18). It is this stage that is often referred to as the sanctification process. It happens by the work of the Holy Spirit in us as we respond to Him. In his letter to the Philippians, Paul phrases it this way: "Therefore, my dear friends, as you have always obeyed—not only in my presence, but now much more in my absence—continue to work out your salvation with fear and trembling, for it is God who works in you to will and to act according to his good purpose" (Phil. 2:12–13). Sanctification occurs because of grace and as an outworking of the grace we received at conversion. It is God working in us to desire and to do His will. It is God working in us to work out our salvation, like the "apple tree" working in the apple seed to work out of it roots and shoots and leaves and the whole new tree. It is the process of our being saved from the power of sin in our lives.

To finish the timeline, the New Testament also speaks of salvation as something that has yet to come, something that culminates in the future. "So Christ was sacrificed once to take away the sins of many people; and he will appear a second time, not to bear sin, but to bring salvation to those who are waiting for him" (Heb. 9:28). Paul urged the Christians in Rome to be motivated by that day: "And do this, understanding the present time. The hour has come for you to wake up from your slumber, because our salvation is nearer now than when we first believed" (Rom. 13:11). This is the day when we will be saved from the presence of sin. One day, heaven and earth will be remade, for as N. T. Wright says in such a wonderfully British way, "The Creator's plan [is] to rescue the world and put it back to rights."[1] All things will be made new. The effects of sin on our universe will be reversed and undone, and the will of God will be perfectly done.

My hunch is that there are many Christians who have been justified, saved by their faith in Christ, but have yet to embrace the Holy Spirit's work of sanctification. That is to say, some of us are like a girl who is engaged for the sheer delight of seeing a ring on her finger but not at all because she is interested in ending her partying days or changing her flirtatious ways. She will still take calls from old boyfriends or chat them up on Facebook. But if marriage is to occur, she must learn to put an end to such foolishness and be "set apart." Whether or not these Christians will end up being saved if no such change occurs is not for me to say. My message is simply that living like that is missing the joy of being engaged. We get engaged because we are choosing to be with a person whom we love deeply. It's a mutual commitment that allows us to fully enjoy another person. And fooling about with other gods is missing the joy of being in covenant with the living God. Peter describes the joy found in our current stage of receiving our salvation:

> *Though you have not seen him, you love him; and even*
> *though you do not see him now, you believe in him and*
> *are filled with an inexpressible and glorious joy, for you are*
> *receiving the goal of your faith, the salvation of your souls.*
> *(1 Peter 1:8–9)*

It is also true, then, that sanctification is about narrowing your options. To say yes to one is to say no a thousand times. The word *sanctification* is stained by angry preachers and harsh sermons about giving up movies and secular music. But to define sanctification by all the things you have to say no to is like defining marriage by all the people you can't develop a connection with: It's true, but it's missing the point. Sanctification, like engagement and marriage, is richest and best when it's ultimately about love.

Make Yourself at Home

A strange thing happens to your money when you get married: It just doesn't seem to go as far. What once was plenty for food and rent and movies and meals out now barely cuts it. Why? Simply because there are new priorities—especially for guys used to the bachelor life. All of a sudden, paper blinds on the windows just won't do. There must be curtains. And if there are curtains, there must be throw pillows to match. And if you're going to do all that, well then, you might as well just paint the walls! And so the money goes. What used to "do" no longer "does."

Then there are all the storage issues. Every newly married man tells me how he's learning to fit all his toiletries in one tiny corner of the under-the-sink cupboard. A man wants a wife, but he underestimates how much room he will have to make for her. Your house is no longer your own.

In a much more dramatic way, the decision to set yourself apart, to become a carrier of God's presence, demands that you make room for Him. As we learned in chapter six, when God moves in, He comes to be in charge. Some things will get rearranged. Some things will get thrown out. Just as a man or woman is willing to lose his or her independence for the sake of sharing life with someone he or she (these double pronouns are getting ridiculous!) loves, it is a love for God that makes us embrace sanctification and all the change that it will bring. Nobody is looking over our shoulder telling us what movies to watch or how often to have a "quiet time" with God. We are set apart. We understand what it means to have God move in and for the love of Him, we would have it no other way.

Then again, this may be the real reason we hesitate to have contact with God for ourselves—we know that our lives will change.
Despite the emotional surge of love we feel every time we're in a
worship service, we understand that love is risky business. So we
develop a sort of business relationship with God. It's a transaction
between two parties who are mutually amicable. We pray a prayer,
go forward to the altar call, do our best to show up at church and
drop something in the bucket, and God keeps us out of hell. It's
okay if He's not our genie, if everything doesn't pan out exactly as
we hoped on earth. We know when it really matters—like on judgment day—He'll do His part. We don't need an emotional high; we
don't need to "sense His presence." We just do our part and He'll
do His. This is a workin' man's Christianity. Leave the conferences
and prayer meetings to the fervent sort. We don't need contact with
God; we just need this contract to work. No big expectation of God,
no big obligation to change on our part. It's a nice relationship with
God. It's sort of like the relationships Patrick Dempsey's character
in *Made of Honor* (my wife made me watch it) fills his life with. He
has elaborate rules for his dating life. Never the same girl two dates
in a row. At least one week before a second date. No dates to a personal event like a family wedding. He's perfected the art of artificial
relationships, gaining all the benefits he wants, and giving up none
of his personal time, space, or commitment.

That is how many of us handle God. We want Him close enough
to get His protection and favor, but not so close that it will prod us
into giving up control, losing independence. Like Israel at Mount
Sinai, we're afraid of getting too close to God. A relationship—
any relationship—demands that we let go, relinquish control, and

lose some independence. As Dempsey's character finds out (okay, I actually liked the movie), having control is not as good as being loved. And the only way to truly let yourself be loved by God is to give up control. You can't have it both ways.

A Long, Bloody Walk

Each story of the ark contains a moment when people realize that they are not in control. When Israel tries to use God like a genie despite their disobedience, He refuses and the battle is lost. They begin understanding that they are not in control and that God will not be used as an instrument of control. Then when the Philistines add the ark to their collection of idols, hoping that the God of Israel would be another god they could manipulate and appease and use to accomplish their goals of wealth and victory, they learned the painful lesson that God does not play those games. He is not a God to be controlled like some pagan deity. Then when the ark is returned and the men of Beth-shemesh decide they can handle the law without the blood, without mercy and grace, they realize that no human has the power to please God. We cannot assert our independence and pretend to be able to impress God. That is yet another attempt at control. Finally, in the David story, the Levites attempted a shortcut to God, using a cart. It resulted in Uzzah trying to handle God, but God will not be handled. He wants contact, not to be handled or controlled.

David started to get the point. After commanding the Levites to set themselves apart and prepare to carry the ark, they began the long-awaited journey, their second attempt to bring God to

Jerusalem. This time, not only was there no cart, there were sacrifices. Samuel's account says that after they had taken six steps, David sacrificed a bull and a fattened calf. The Chronicles account says that "because God was clearly helping the Levites as they carried the Ark ... they sacrificed seven bulls and seven rams" (1 Chron. 15:26 NLT). Some suggest the sacrifices continued every six steps. Either way, I imagine it was tremendously inconvenient, not to mention messy.

There is a truth at work here. When we accept God's offer and choose to embark on a journey of firsthand faith, we are setting ourselves apart, enrolling in a lifelong process of sanctification. What we learn early in that process is that this road to knowing God is covered in the blood of sacrifice. As *The Message* translates Jesus' words:

> *Don't look for shortcuts to God. The market is flooded with surefire, easygoing formulas for a successful life that can be practiced in your spare time. Don't fall for that stuff, even though crowds of people do. The way to life—to God!—is vigorous and requires total attention. (Matt. 7:13–14 MSG)*

We keep looking for shortcuts to God, and all the while He keeps inviting us on a long, bloody walk.

First, it is the blood of Christ Himself, by whose blood we are clean, free, righteous, able to stand before God. Second, it is the blood of our sacrifice. But let me be clear: Everything we need to be accepted by God is in the blood of Christ. Nothing about our sacrifice makes God love us more. Our sacrifice is simply our worship—our love response to God. Paul makes this clear in Romans 12:1: "Therefore, I urge you, brothers, in view of God's mercy, to offer your bodies as living sacrifices, holy and pleasing to God—this is your spiritual act of worship."

The word he uses for *worship*—or as some translations say it, *service*—is the word Paul used earlier to describe Jewish temple worship: the ritual and practice of animal sacrifices. The Greek translation of the Old Testament—the Septuagint—also uses this word (*latreia*) to describe priestly temple service. It seems Paul is trying to say that our new way of worshipping, the new "temple worship," is the laying down of our lives, the offering of our hearts in surrender. What's more, this "new way to worship" is a response to God's love and mercy. "In view of God's mercy," Romans 12:1 begins. Earlier in this same letter to the Romans, Paul spells out how we know God's love:

> *But God demonstrates his own love for us in this: While we were still sinners, Christ died for us. Since we have now been justified by his blood, how much more shall we be saved from God's wrath through him! For if, when we were God's enemies, we were reconciled to him through the death of his Son, how much more, having been reconciled, shall we be saved through his life! (Rom. 5:8–10)*

God showed His love by dying for us while we were sinners, His very enemies. In light of such love, our response can only be the laying down of our lives. Worship has always been about sacrifice; now it is about the living sacrifice of our lives, given in response to God's love. To Paul, sacrifice isn't about gritting your teeth or clenching your fists; it's about opening your hands and giving up control. It's about lovingly letting go.

Profiles

Cameron is not a pastor. Neither is Roxanne. Or Mark.

Cameron is a pilot in the United States Air Force. He flies C-17s, fuel and transport planes large enough to fit a tank in the main cargo area. I met Cameron when he was a cadet in the Air Force Academy here in Colorado Springs. He married a wonderful girl that graduated from New Life School of Worship—our ministry training school at New Life. Cameron met Marelize on a mission trip sponsored by theMILL, New Life's college ministry. Not long after graduating from the Academy, Cameron and Marelize got married. I was his third-best man. (There were two others who were chosen before me but neither could make it to the wedding—such is the life of military servicemen.) Cameron did his pilot training in unspectacular Enid, Oklahoma, and is now based in lush and beautiful Tacoma, Washington.

But there's more. A year ago, Cameron decided to form a sort of "board of directors" for his life. He chose godly men that he respected and asked them to speak into his life and help him grow. At the beginning of the year, Cameron e-mailed me some goals for the different areas of his life, putting in practical form the emotional and spiritual desires in his heart. There's no guilt from falling short nor pride for meeting the mark. It's simply his way of responding to God's work in his life. He's an avid reader and a lifelong learner.

His ability to synthesize and integrate what he learns is astounding. While he's adding knowledge about investing and marketing and good leadership practices, the focus of his learning is unmistakably God and His Word.

Roxanne is a farmwife and has been for over thirty years. Early in her marriage they lived in California, but they soon returned to Iowa when Bill decided to take over the family farm. The town down the road from their farm has about one thousand people, approximately ten churches, one school they share with the next town over, and no stoplights. Roxanne spent roughly two decades raising, caring for, and investing in her two daughters, one of whom I had the joy of marrying.

Roxanne never went to seminary, and as of now, is not ordained. But she loves the Bible. She reads it, studies it, devours it with a passion. She has slowly built a small library of study tools like concordances and Bible dictionaries. She has learned over the years not to just believe something a preacher said, even if he or she is on TV. She has learned to search it out for herself. With Bereanlike diligence, she tests ideas by the light of the Word of God she has grown to love. Whenever she comes to visit or whenever we head to the farm, she seems to find a way to draw me into a lengthy discourse on some theological question or biblical exegesis. (okay, the "lengthy" part is my fault. I tend to talk. A lot.)

Mark is a rising star in the business world. Since taking a job with Tyson Food about five years ago, he has gotten two or three major promotions and earned the trust of his bosses. Even though sales is not Mark's passion, he knows how to work hard and learn quickly. Mark was a tall, fast wide receiver at Northwestern College in Orange City, Iowa, where he met Bill and Roxanne's other daughter, Abby.

After they got married and moved to Arkansas for Mark's job, Mark wasted no time in finding a good church and getting plugged in. Despite required travel and the often-demanding pressure of his job, Mark is part of a men's small group that meets every Wednesday at six in the morning. He is committed to learn about and to grow in Christ. And both he and his wife are better for it.

You can't measure spiritual growth by the services you attend or the frequency with which you read your Bible. In fact, as I pointed out in the last chapter, those things can become a "cart"—a convenient substitute for our own living relationship with God. But they can also be the signs of devotion, the marks of sanctification and sacrifice, the evidence of a life yearning to be in contact with God. So what's the difference? Love. Because I know each of these people well, I know why they have formed these habits in their lives. Their behavior is not an attempt to please God with their efforts. It is to reinforce their desire for God. It is the fruit of their surrender to the Holy Spirit's work in them. I know this because I know them.

Cameron, Roxanne, and Mark are not pastors. They are not the ones you would call "God experts" or "God professionals." They are Christians. They understand that they were made for contact with God. They believe they were redeemed so that contact is now possible. And so they live set apart, like one engaged to the love of her life. They exist as living sacrifices, lovingly surrendering in response to God's love, "in view of God's mercy" (Rom. 12:1). They are ordinary people not content with an ordinary, workmanlike relationship with God. No carts here. Christianity is a contact sport.

DISCUSSION QUESTIONS:

1. "Having control is not as good as being loved." How have you held on to control and missed out on being fully loved by God?

2. Have you experienced taking a "long, bloody walk with God"? Describe it.

3. How does your love for God lead you to live in more "contact" with Him?

11. Invitation

The last two years of my life have been about change. Three years ago I had a different pastor as a boss, a head full of optimism, a heart tainted with pride, and a relationship with God that was adequate yet somewhat aloof. Today, I have a new pastor I am growing to love and dreams mitigated by suffering and tragedy yet buoyed by an eternal hope. But something is different in my heart as well.

It's hard to describe or quantify. I know a new depth of brokenness beyond what I've ever known. I know firsthand how unpredictable, how out of our control, life is.

I was standing in the parking lot switching out the car seats from our van to our other car when I heard the sound. It was a loud metallic boom that reverberated in the cool December air. At first I thought it was a giant light truss falling on a stage. It sounded like it came from the outside of the Tent, our semipermanent structure on the east side of our campus where the junior high met on Sundays. I reached for my phone to call my buddy Jared Newman, the junior-high youth pastor, to see what ruckus he and his kids were up to. I realized I had left my phone in the sanctuary. Then the sound came again. And then another. The thought crossed my mind that it could be gunshots and I wouldn't even know it. I was unfamiliar with the sound.

More sounds, this time in succession. I walked a little toward the Tent to see what might be going on. Then I saw a couple run within the fenced-off area on the north side of the Tent, ducking for cover. Something was wrong.

Suddenly the side doors of the main hallway burst open in front of me and someone screamed, "There's a shooter! There's a shooter!"

I froze. *My wife and my two little girls are in there!*

The next few minutes felt like an eternity. My head was clouded. I started to head toward the doors. Members of our staff urged me not to go in.

No, no. Glenn, you can't go back in!

But my family is in there!

My wife was waiting in our offices with our two daughters. Sophia was two and a half; Norah was barely a year old.

People were scrambling through the exits, ducking, crouching, covering their heads with their hands. Without really thinking, I got in my car to be ready for a quick getaway in case at any moment Holly and our girls ran out. I was scanning the clusters of people quickly dispersing in the parking lot when a woman asked if I could

take her to her car. I told her to get in but that I wasn't going anywhere without my family. Soon another woman, an acquaintance
of this other lady, asked if she could jump in too. I agreed. My head
was a mess of thoughts. Then I saw Landon, a friend and one of the
musicians in our band.

"Landon! Let me borrow your phone! I need to call Holly …
she's still in there!"

He handed me his phone. My fingers felt clumsier than normal
as I struggled to dial her number. No answer. It was sent to voice
mail. My car was turned away from the doors toward the exit, per-
pendicular from Landon's car as the call ended. Just then one of the
women in the car said, "Hey, there's a young mom running out of
the building with two kids!"

I knew it was Holly. I turned the car around in time to see Holly
running out of the doors with one child under each arm, holding
them almost parallel to the ground. It felt like a scene from a movie.
In a second, I had pulled up to the curb. Without thinking, I told the
ladies to get out of my car so I could get my family in. In retrospect,
it was needlessly panicky and a little thoughtless. We could have
crammed everyone in despite the car seats in the back row that they
would have had to squeeze between. But I wasn't thinking straight.
As it was, Holly jumped in the front seat with Sophia and Norah
held closely against her, and we drove off.

Fortunately the women who had taken shelter in my car were
fine. Shortly after we left the parking lot, word came that the
shooter was suspected to be down. When I pulled up to my driveway, Landon was there to check on us, like a good friend. He was
fine and so were we.

Inside our house, we sat shaking in front of the TV as we watched reporters try to explain what we had just seen. The Broncos were playing the Chiefs. It was a big game, and I had been looking forward to relaxing on my couch and watching it after church. Now it just seemed silly.

What had just happened?

Holly told me how she heard the sounds while she was waiting alone in the offices of our worship ministry. Like a good farm girl, she recognized them as gunshots. She grabbed our girls and hid under the desk in the deepest corner of the small office bay. In a rare moment of complete obedience, our girls lay still and silent. As the gunshots sounded like they were getting closer, Holly heard a voice inside urging her to get out *now*. She peeked through the side windows by the main office door, and the side hallway seemed clear. She made a dash for the exit, saw my car, and seconds later we were driving away.

The moments that followed were a mix of relief, panic, and sheer disbelief. *Thank God we're okay. Was anyone harmed? Any dead? What just happened?*

It was later that day that we heard the tragic news that Rachel and Stephanie Works, sisters who had been very involved in our student ministries, had been killed. Rachel was sixteen; Stephanie was eighteen. They are survived by their father, David, mother, Marie, and sisters, Laurie and Grace. Over the months that followed, I had several conversations with David, listening to his grief, his struggle, and his family's remarkable faith through all of it. Their story is told at length in their book, *Gone In a Heartbeat*, so I will not tell it here.

Through the shock of scandal and the tragedy of a shooting, the faith of our church has been rocked, refined, and reinforced. And for me—for me personally—I am learning to trust a loving God, completely. The world is not at my fingertips; power is an illusion, as it always has been. I have been part of the leadership of a church that was, so to speak, at the "top of its game." I have seen that same church broken, in tears, by the sin of its leader. I have traveled in the name of our church and been warmly received all over the world because of our reputation. And I have also heard the shots of an angry gunman who hated us and everything we stand for. In some way, I have experienced abundance and have been abased. Through all of it I have learned that I am not in control. But more than that, I am convinced of this: God is faithful. I am learning to fall back into the arms of a God who is stronger, wiser, and more loving than I could ever imagine.

Seeing Again

There's a song I had written about a year before everything unraveled. It was written in a time of peace, but it was a gift for a time of turmoil to come. By the time the *My Savior Lives* album came out, New Life Church was a month into the uncertain waters of transition following the release of our founding pastor. Ross Parsley, my dear friend and the longtime worship pastor at New Life, rose to the occasion as interim pastor and called early-morning prayer meetings during the week. It was in these meetings that the songs from the CD took on profound meaning. They gave us new hope as we began to lift our hearts to God. This song is just one among many that carried us during those dark winter months.

One thing I know that I have found
Through all the troubles that surround
You are the Rock that never fails
You never fail

One thing I know that I believe
Through every blessing I receive
You are the only One that stays
You always stay

You never change
You're still the same
You are the everlasting God

You will remain
After the day has gone and the things of earth have past
Everlasting God[1]

In each story of the ark that we have unpacked in this book, there has been an unexpected turn of events, an unforeseen hitch in the plans. I have called these moments—both in these stories and in our lives—"what the heck?" moments. For some, it is too irreverent; for others, not irreverent enough for the depth of the pain, shock, or sorrow. Regardless of what you call it or what you exclaim, it is a moment where our view of God is challenged. It can be an occasion to walk away from God or an opportunity to engage Him, to wrestle with Him. As we choose the latter, we begin to see again.

Without attempting to solve the problem of pain, we can at least recognize that pain is often the backdrop for a rediscovery of God. Whether that is true as a result of God's design or whether it is simply a picture of His redemption, God is always at work—"in all things" (Rom. 8:28)—for our good and His glory. It is God who is always calling, inviting, ever wooing us to Himself.

Dance, Dance

We were made to be loved by God and to love Him. I love the way historian George Marsden summarizes the thoughts and ideas of the great Jonathan Edwards about why God created us:

> *Why would such an infinitely good, perfect, and eternal being create? … The ultimate reason that God creates, said Edwards, is not to remedy some lack in God, but to extend that perfect internal communication of the triune God's goodness and love.… God's joy and happiness and delight in divine perfections is expressed externally by communicating that happiness and delight to created beings.… The universe is an explosion of God's glory. Perfect goodness, beauty, and love radiate from God and draw creatures to ever increasingly share in the Godhead's joy and delight.… The ultimate end of creation, then, is union in love between God and loving creatures.*[2]

The universe is an explosion of God's glory. Wow. The love within the Trinity—the tri-personal God who is a union in communion or a communion in union—exploded outward, choosing to

create a universe, to set humanity as the crown of all creation, and
to invite us in. God created us as objects of His affection. We were
made for love.

The Greek church fathers used the term *perichoresis* to describe
the relationship within the Trinity. *Peri* is the word for "around"
and *choresis* is the root from which we get words like "choreogra-
phy." The two taken together—"perichoresis"—communicates the
idea of movement around, and even something like a Great Dance.
Borrowing that idea, C. S. Lewis elaborates:

> *And that ... is the most important difference between Christian-
> ity and all other religions: that in Christianity God is not a static
> thing—not even a person—but a dynamic, pulsating activity, a
> life, almost a kind of drama. Almost, if you will not think me
> irreverent, a kind of dance....*
>
> *And now, what does it all matter? It matters more than any-
> thing else in the world. The whole dance, or drama ... is to be
> played out in each one of us: or (putting it the other way round)
> each one of us has got to ... take his place in that dance.*[3]

There is a Great Dance within the Godhead, and we have been
invited in. Sin had separated us, doomed us to be distant. But Jesus,
almost as if He left the dance briefly, somehow mysteriously and super-
naturally became a man, making "himself nothing, taking the very
nature of a servant" while on earth (Phil. 2:7). Jesus took all our sins
upon Himself, bore the full wrath of God for us, and died on that cross.
When He rose again, it became official: Death had been swallowed up
by life, sin would no longer have the last word. Love had won.

And so Jesus stands at the door of our hearts knocking. If we will but open ourselves, admit that we are nothing without Him, doomed to die unless we take in His life, then Jesus comes into us and brings us into the love—the dance—of the Godhead.

Jesus, praying before the cross, anticipates this:

> *My prayer is not for them alone. I pray also for those who will believe in me through their message, that all of them may be one, Father, just as you are in me and I am in you. May they also be in us so that the world may believe that you have sent me. I have given them the glory that you gave me, that they may be one as we are one: I in them and you in me. (John 17:20–23)*

Why is it that in order to truly have life we must be *in* God? Is it some sort of catch, a sales tool on a cosmic scale, that in order to get what we need most—life—we must give up what we love most—our control or independence? No. It is simply the way God is. C. S. Lewis, in what follows his description of the "dance" we are invited to join, says it this way:

> *There is no other way to the happiness for which we were made. Good things as well as bad … are caught by a kind of infection. If you want to get warm you must stand near the fire: if you want to be wet you must get into the water. If you want joy, power, peace, eternal life, you must get close to, or even into, the thing that has them. They are not a sort of prize which God could, if He chose, just hand out to anyone. They*

are a fountain of energy and beauty spurting up at the centre [sic] of reality. If you are close to it, the spray will wet you: if you are not, you will remain dry. Once a man is united to God, how could he not live forever? Once a man is separated from God, what can he do but whither and die?

But how is he to be united to God? How is it possible for us to be taken into the three-Personal life? ...

Now the whole offer which Christianity makes is this: that we can, if we let God have His way, come to share in the life of Christ.[4]

Worship

There is only one way to respond to the glorious invitation we have been offered by God. It is not to repay or to earn or to work hard.

I have heard so many preachers take the approach of heaping guilt onto their listeners, saying things like, "Jesus died for you; the least you could do is live for Him!" Even the great Keith Green, whose music and life story have deeply impacted me, sang the phrase, "Jesus rose from the grave and you can't even get out of bed!" The universal tendency in believers everywhere seems to be to respond to God's grace with our own work and effort. Even now, as you finish this book, you may be struggling with what you should do next, how you can work harder, be better, read your Bible more, or do some other Christian duty you have neglected that needs more attention.

To be sure, the Christian life requires effort. In the words of George MacDonald, "God is easy to please but hard to satisfy."[5] The illustration MacDonald paired with that phrase is of a child learning to walk. No parent with any sense would chastise a little toddler who falls while trying to walk for the first time. I think of the times when Sophia and Norah began to take their first steps. Each was different in their approach. Sophia was cautious and tentative; Norah was more willing to stumble ahead. We've got video footage of each of them, but none of our ridiculous faces, silly with glee. We cheered them on for the smallest independent step. When they were able to make it five paces, we congratulated them like Olympians. We were, indeed, easy to please. But no parent would feel all right with a ten-year-old who insisted on crawling from place to place. Learning to walk is good for a toddler, but eventually a child must grow to run. In a similar way, God is pleased with our response, our movement toward Him. But He will not be satisfied until we have become like Him.

So effort is required. Yet even this effort, as we pointed out in chapter ten, is still the result of God's work in us. If it were dependent on us, it would not be just difficult but impossible. And our effort cannot be an attempt to earn God's favor or to repay Him for His love. Such a response to God's marvelous invitation will simply not do.

The best word I can use to describe a life of responding to God, of accepting His invitations, of drawing near, making room for Him to work, yielding to His will, and cooperating with the Holy Spirit is this: worship. Yes, worship is ascribing worth, honor, and glory to God. And yes, as Matt Redman has summed up, worship is a response to a revelation of who God is.[6] Worship is about sacrifice—a surrender to God out of a faith in who He is. And all of it is wrapped up in love. It is at its core loving God because He has first loved us.

But worship plays out in our lives, beyond the worship service, in how we live. To really grasp the relationship that is offered to us through Christ, we must think of the Christian life not as work, but as worship. Worship is the language of love, and it is the only way to respond to the love we have been shown.

Imagine being invited to the White House for a private dinner with the president and his family. You open the mail one day to find a beautiful cream envelope marked with a special seal. As you read the invitation, you can't help but yell out the incredible news to your spouse and kids: "The president wants to have dinner with us ... our family!" After reading and rereading it, you mark the date on every calendar you can find and then start sharing the good news with friends and family—partly rejoicing, partly bragging. But what if, as the day got closer, you got nervous and decided you needed to do something more in the meantime? Imagine updating your resume, hoping to impress Mr. President with your degree and all your job experience. Imagine printing it out, and mailing it to the White House. What if you started to send gifts to the president? Ties, socks, ball caps, and watches. What if you did all of that and then on the day of the dinner you simply didn't show up?

It sounds foolish, doesn't it? Why send in your resume when he has already invited you? Obviously he knows enough about you to invite you and your family to a private dinner. Why the gifts? Can you really repay the honor you've been given by the invitation? And besides, what could he need from you? The only way to respond to a dinner invitation is to show up. You could come with a gift, but, above all else, *come.*

The only way to respond to God's invitation to draw near is worship.

DISCUSSION QUESTIONS:

1. How is it helpful to visualize the Trinity as a great, joyful dance that we have been invited into?

2. If "worship is the language of love," how do we worship God as a response to His invitation?

12. Joy

I wear a few different hats. So do you. The nature of our jobs and lives these days requires us to play many different roles.

I'm a husband.

I'm a father.

I'm a son.

I'm a worship leader.

Songwriter.

Preacher.

Writer.

Manager.

Coach.

Teacher.

Yet only a few of these roles are irreplaceable. The truth is someone else can lead worship for the services under my care. Someone else can preach, teach, write, manage, coach, or write songs. There were others before me, and there will be many after I'm gone. But I am the only one that can be a husband to my wife. No one else can be the father to my girls. I am the only son my parents have. All my functional roles are expendable, completely replaceable. It is my relational roles that are the irreplaceable ones.

Even beyond those, there is one relational, irreplaceable role that is eternally sacred, that no human in history can fill: my role as a child of God. There are a million angels who sing God's praise, but only I can love God as the child He created and redeemed. Someone else can serve Him and do the things He has given me to do, as important as those things are. But no one else can give Him my love, my worship.

David understood at least a little bit of this. In Psalm 27, he prayed, "One thing I ask of the LORD, this is what I seek: that I may dwell in the house of the LORD all the days of my life, to gaze upon the beauty of the LORD and to seek him in his temple" (Ps. 27:4).

Of all the privileges David had as king, going into the tabernacle before the ark was not supposed to be one of them. That was the role of the priest. But David couldn't take it. That was the one thing he really wanted. He didn't care about his position or the privilege of his role. His role as king was replaceable. There would be other kings. But there would be no other king who would be allowed in before the ark to worship the way David did.[1] That was the result of David's singular passion for God. It was David's one thing.

Hundreds of years later, Jesus, addressing the busy, complaining Martha, said, "Martha, Martha … you are worried and upset about many things, but only one thing is needed. Mary has chosen what is better, and it will not be taken away from her" (Luke 10:41–42).

Martha was trying to be a good hostess, an important thing in that culture. It was a necessary role. Mary, on the other hand, chose to ignore her obligations, her other roles and duties. She chose to sit at Jesus' feet. Jesus made it clear that of all the tasks that needed to be done, of all the roles both women could have or should have played, there was only one role that was needed. Only one role could not be taken away. It was what Mary chose. Sitting at Jesus' feet is an irreplaceable role. It was Mary's one thing.

A few decades later, the apostle Paul wrote a manifesto of his own spiritual pilgrimage.

I want to know Christ and the power of his resurrection and the fellowship of sharing in his sufferings, becoming like him in his death, and so, somehow, to attain to the resurrection from the dead. Not that I have already obtained all this, or have already been made perfect, but I press on to take hold of that for which Christ Jesus took hold of me. Brothers, I do not consider myself yet to have taken hold of it. But one thing I do: Forgetting what is behind and straining toward what is ahead, I press on toward the goal to win the prize for which God has called me heavenward in Christ Jesus. (Phil. 3:10–14)

What Paul wanted more than anything else was to know Christ, to become like Him. I imagine Paul was not a guy with a lot of "margins" in his schedule. Anyone who describes his life as a "drink being poured out" is probably a busy man. Paul had a lot of things to do. Yet the thing he made central to his life—the pursuit that defined all other pursuits—was his straining toward the goal of knowing Jesus. It was Paul's one thing.

David. Mary. Paul. They could have defined their lives by many things—David by his position or fame or influence; Mary by her responsibilities or duties; Paul by the churches he planted or the letters he penned. Each had many roles that they played. Yet each of them understood that only one role was sacred and irreplaceable. It is the one thing desired, the one thing needed, the one thing to be done. It is knowing Jesus.

The more we hear God's call and respond in love and worship, the more we hear God's call. And on and on it goes. That is exactly what the last few years have been for me. I have returned again to "do the things [I] did at first" (Rev. 2:5). My heart is soft. Alive. I am learning to hold the things I do more loosely. Anything can change. And if it does, it does not matter as much as it used to. I am not defined any longer by the church I serve or the things I've accomplished—be they little or great. I am defined by the invitation, by the love that calls my name, and by the joy I find in response.

Every day is another step in the journey. Like a child, I may stumble as I walk, but my Father is in front of me. I am heading His way. I have finally realized all the big and small ways I was relying on secondhand information, letting others do the heavy lifting of faith for me. And I am finally convinced that no one can know God for me. Of all my roles, all my tasks, all my pursuits, there must be one thing I desire, one thing I need, one thing I do: Engage God firsthand.

"Burning" Beginnings

I admit I once lived by rumors of you; now I have it all firsthand—from my own eyes and ears! I'm sorry—forgive me. I'll never do that again, I promise! I'll never again live on crusts of hearsay, crumbs of rumor. (Job 42:5–6 MSG)

It was late 2007 when I first read those words. I had been reading the book of Job in *The Message*—appropriate when you're living through a "what the heck?" moment!—and was struck by how well the phrase captured the journey I was on. The seeds of a song began with a prechorus. I hastily forced the song to a finish and even played it in that form a few times at theMILL. But it wasn't quite right. Actually, it wasn't even close.

Almost a year later, Gregg Hampton, a friend and former student at New Life School of Worship, came to visit. I played him the prechorus, the only part of the song I really loved. He played me a chorus that he had been messing around with but never found verses for. It was perfect. We ran inside, leaving the grill briefly unattended, and scribbled out verses in the magic of the moment. After several rounds under the microscope, we created a song that best captures the Lord's work in my heart over these past few years:

The faith of yesterday is all I had inside
I have seen it fade and all my love run dry

I have only heard the whisper of Your majesty
All I've known were only rumors
Now my eyes have seen Your glory, God

You are the one that set me on fire
Everything is burning in me
You are my love, You're all I desire
Everything is burning in me

Consuming every part, my heart has come alive
Now I know that I am yours, a sacrifice
I have only heard the whisper of Your majesty
All I've known were only rumors
Now my eyes have seen Your glory, God

Hallelujah! Everything is burning
Everything is burning in me[2]

MapQuest

Now, I hope you see, at last, that the reason God wants to strip away
our rumors of Him, the reason He wants us to know Him firsthand,
to have a faith that engages Him and wrestles with Him through the
dark hours of the night, is because when we know Him, when we
have contact with Him, we come alive. God revealed Himself to Job
not to explain the situation or the reasons or the Devil's wager. God
meets with Job at the end of the story to be His salvation. Job was
saved from wrongheaded, small-minded notions of God—"crumbs

of rumor," as he called it. He now had it all firsthand, seeing with his own eyes.

The driving force behind God's quest to open our eyes is not some urge for theological correctness; it is His love for us. He knows that our highest good and His ultimate glory come from the same thing: our joy in God. John Piper has written extensively and profoundly about this, calling himself a Christian hedonist. Echoing C. S. Lewis's famous words, Piper argues that God finds our desires not too strong but too weak.[3] We are too easily pleased with the things in this world that we have called "joys," when they are but shadows, hints at the greatest joy of all—the joy that comes from being in a living relationship with God. And nothing glorifies God more than our realizing, recognizing, and acknowledging God as the ultimate joy.

Good doctrine is important. But it is not an end in itself. Getting us to think correctly about God is like teaching a man to read a map correctly before he embarks on a journey. But what family enters the address of their destination into MapQuest, plotting out their summer road trip, and then prints out the map and goes to sleep, reflecting on what a great vacation it was? That is foolishness. The map is for the journey.

All our discussion up until this point has helped erase the faulty lines we have drawn on our map, obscuring the markings of the true path. We have been like a child who scribbles mindlessly on a document that is too important for him to grasp. And God, sometimes against our wish, finds a way to get the crayon out of our hands and gently teaches us what it is we have defaced. We have disfigured truth and distorted the revelation of God that He has given to us through

Jesus and through His Word. We have fashioned a god in our own image, one that we can control. We have taken information second-hand, and traveled down shortcuts that have proven to be dead ends. Slowly, the map is cleaned up, the rumors are dispelled, and the road is clear again. Now it is time to use the map for its intended purpose: a journey.

You may have seen a map of Colorado. It may even have been a topographical one, using colors to mark the different elevations, outlining the great Rocky Mountains. But I can tell you, there is nothing like driving through the Colorado mountains for yourself. As I write this, the leaves are about to change colors. Next month, I will head west on I-70, wind my way up Berthoud Pass, and make my way to Winter Park for theMILL's annual fall retreat. Though I am deathly afraid of mountain driving, especially when there is any hint of precipitation—which October always seems to have—I will take the journey. With every white-knuckled grip of my steering wheel, I will make turn after turn, breathless from fear and from wonder of the beauty around me. Finally, I will pull into the spectacular Crooked Creek Young Life camp and see lightly snowcapped peaks with a skirt of yellow and red trees just above the valley. This is a beauty I cannot see from a map. This is a spectacle I cannot grasp from pictures or turn-by-turn directions. This is a sight that can only be seen by taking the journey.

There is love that has made you, that has come to redeem and rescue you, that is calling you to come. Wonder, beauty, life in all its fullness awaits you. The fear of the switchbacks and hairpin turns can't compare with the sight that awaits. The miracle of the tri-personal God is that not only is God the One drawing us, it is also

God in us and with us that helps us in our journey, and it is God that is the road—or as Jesus said, "the Way"—along which we travel. God is in all of it. Love made us, love calls us, love is the way.

Jesus, for the joy set before Him, endured the cross. In similar fashion, we for the joy of knowing Christ set before us embrace the vigorous, lifelong journey of firsthand faith. Our discussion here has ended. But your journey has just begun. Are you ready?

DISCUSSION QUESTIONS:

1. A journey requires a good map. How has your "map"—your view of God—been challenged or cleaned up by reading this book?

2. In what ways will you live out this journey by God's grace?

Notes

Chapter 1

[1] Tobias Wolff, *Old School* (New York: Vintage Books, 2003), 15.

[2] Henri Nouwen, *In the Name of Jesus* (New York: Crossroad, 1989), 19–20.

[3] Henri Nouwen, *In the Name of Jesus*, 20.

[4] C. S. Lewis, *The Problem of Pain* (New York: Touchstone, 1996), 83.

Chapter 2

[1] Robert Mitchell, "It's Just the Key to Your Room," *Computerworld*, January 16, 2006, www.computerworld.com (accessed February 13, 2009).

Chapter 3

[1] David Goetz, *Death by Suburb* (New York: HarperCollins, 2006), 9.

[2] Chip Heath and Dan Heath, *Made to Stick* (New York: Random House, 2008), 67.

[3] Chip Heath and Dan Heath, *Made to Stick*, 68.

[4] Philip Yancey, *The Bible Jesus Read* (Grand Rapids, MI: Zondervan, 1999), 36–37.

5   Elie Wiesel and Robert Franciosi, *Conversations* (Jackson: University Press of Mississippi, 2002), 87.

6   Ed Vitagliano, "Christianity growing in staggering fashion in Africa, Latin America and Asia," *Christian Post,* April 20, 2004, www.christianpost.com (accessed February 13, 2009).

7   W. E. Vine, Merril F. Unger, and William White Jr., *Vine's Complete Expository Bible Dictionary of Old and New Testament Words* (Nashville, TN: Thomas Nelson, 1996), 142.

8   Vine, Unger, and White Jr., *Vine's Expository Bible Dictionary,* 142.

Chapter 4

1   Derek Burnett, "Life after Hurricane Katrina," *Reader's Digest,* August 2006, www.rd.com (accessed January 30, 2009).

2   Ibid.

3   Joni Mitchell, "Big Yellow Taxi," *Ladies of the Canyon* © 1970 Reprise Records.

4   C. S. Lewis, *The Weight of Glory* (New York: HarperCollins, 2001), 26.

5   Lewis, *The Problem of Pain,* 86 (see chap. 1, n. 4).

6   Ibid., 87.

7   Ibid., 85.

Chapter 5

1   Associated Press, "Welker refocused after 'dagger to the heart' from Giants," *USA Today,* June 29, 2008, www.usatoday.com/sports/football/nfl/patriots/2008-06-29-welker_N.htm (accessed January 30, 2009).

2   Author unknown, "Dagon," www.wikipedia.com (accessed January 30, 2009).

3   Garrison Keillor, *Pontoon* (New York: Penguin Group, 2007), 226.

Chapter 6

1   Ernest Becker, *Escape From Evil* (New York: Free Press, 1985), quoted in Goetz, *Death by Suburb*, 41–42 (see chap. 3, n. 1).

2   David Goetz, *Death by Suburb*, 43

3   Ibid.

4   Second Kings 10:28–30 is an example of a "godly king"—Jehu, who destroyed Baal worship but didn't undo Jeroboam's sin; 2 Kings 13:5–7 gives Jehoahaz as another example.

5   Susan Olasky, "An Old Deception," *WORLD Magazine*, June 28, 2008, 60.

6   Rhonda Byrne, "The Secret," The Secret: Official Web Site, www.thesecret.tv (accessed January 30, 2009).

Chapter 7

1   The ark of the covenant was commonly referred to as the "ark of Testimony," so it seems that these other items were placed in front of it, though not necessarily *in* it—at least at this point.

2   "There was nothing in the ark except the two stone tablets that Moses had placed in it at Horeb, where the LORD made a covenant with the Israelites after they came out of Egypt" (1 Kings 8:9).

3   Vine, Unger, and White Jr., *Vine's Expository Bible Dictionary*, 470 (see chap. 3, n. 7); Merril Unger, *The New Unger's Bible Dictionary* (Chicago: Moody Press, 1988), 997.

4   Unger, *The New Unger's Bible Dictionary*, 998-99.

[5] Justo Gonzales, *The Story of Christianity, Vol. 1* (New York: HarperCollins, 1984), 214.

Chapter 8

[1] Andrew Delbanco, *The Real American Dream: A Meditation on Hope* (Cambridge, MA: Harvard University Press, 2000), quoted in Timothy Keller, *The Reason for God* (New York: Dutton / Penguin Group, 2008), 161.

[2] Ibid.

[3] Sam Thielman, "Gone Batty," *WORLD Magazine* 23, no. 15 (2008): 17.

[4] Miroslav Volf, *Exclusion and Embrace: A Theological Exploration of Identity, Otherness, and Reconciliation* (Nashville: Abingdon, 1996), 303–4.

[5] John Stott, *The Cross of Christ* (Downer's Grove, IL: InterVarsity Press, 1986), 160.

[6] C. S. Lewis, *Mere Christianity*, (New York: Touchstone / Simon & Schuster, 1980), 168-70.

[7] Ibid., 183.

[8] Ibid., 183.

[9] Ibid., 53.

[10] Ibid., 54.

Chapter 9

[1] James F. White, *A Brief History of Christian Worship* (Nashville: Abingdon, 1993), 47.

[2] Ibid.

[3] Ibid., 55.

Chapter 10

[1] N. T. Wright, *Simply Christian* (New York: HarperCollins, 2006), 10.

Chapter 11

[1] Glenn Packiam, "Everlasting God," *My Savior Lives* © 2006, Vertical Worship/Integrity Music.

[2] George Marsden, *Jonathan Edwards: A Life* (New Haven, CT: Yale University Press, 2003), 462-63.

[3] Lewis, *Mere Christianity*, 152-53 (see chap. 8, n. 6).

[4] Ibid., 153.

[5] George MacDonald, quoted in ibid., 174.

[6] Matt Redman, *Facedown* (Ventura, CA: Regal, 2004), 96.

Chapter 12

[1] The tabernacle of David had only one item of furniture: the ark itself. In 2 Samuel 12, after his sin with Bathsheba, David goes into the house of the Lord to worship. It seems very likely that he was before the ark itself since there were no other items in the tent—unlike in Moses' tabernacle, which had chambers, as the temple eventually would.

[2] Glenn Packiam and Gregg Hampton, "Burning in Me," Rumors and Revelations 2009 Vertical Worship/Integrity Music.

[3] John Piper, *Desiring God: Meditations of a Christian Hedonist* (Sisters, OR: Multnomah, 1986), 99.

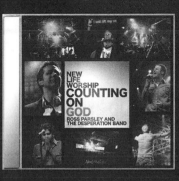